BEATING THE BANKS

Morris Kaplan is a Sydney-based finance journalist who has had fifteen years' experience as a stockbroker and investment adviser. He has written extensively on business, finance and investment for a number of publications, including the *Australian Financial Review* and *Corporate Review*.

As a stockbroker, Kaplan provided financial planning and investment advice for private investors and large corporations, including FAI and Telstra. He also had numerous dealings with Australia's major banks, which has given him the insight and depth to write about what really goes on in the heads of our financial institutions.

His unique position as a former corporate player turned journalist has given him a privileged vantage point from which to explore the psychology of banks, and to make the person in the street aware of what he or she really needs to know.

BEATING THE BANKS

How to Fight Back, Take Control and Make a Profit

MORRIS KAPLAN

MANDARIN

Published 1997 by Mandarin
a part of Reed Books Australia
35 Cotham Road, Kew 3101
a division of Reed International Books Australia Pty Limited

Typeset in Times by J&M Typesetting
Printed and bound in Australia by Australian Print Group

National Library of Australia
cataloguing-in-publication data:

Kaplan, Morris, 1947– .
Beating the banks: how to fight back, take control and make a profit.

Bibliography.
Includes index.
ISBN 1 86330 620 X

1. Banks and banking. I. Title.

332.1

To Ruth, my partner and soul mate

Acknowledgements

Beating the Banks is replete with rich stories from friends, former clients and people I did not know. I am indebted to them for agreeing to be interviewed and giving all of us the benefit of their experiences.

I thank my agent, David Holland, for the discussion that led to this book and my publisher, Deb Callaghan, for taking the chance with me.

Thank you also to my very instructive editors, Edward Caruso and Judy Brookes, who guided me painlessly through an otherwise tortuous process.

I am grateful to CRAA for the use of sample pages from a credit report, and Australians for Banking Justice for permission to reproduce material from their newsletter, *Victims News*.

Contents

Preface

I remember the Commonwealth Bank representative visiting my primary school to empty my money box — the one shaped like the bank's Gothic headquarters in Martin Place, Sydney. This event took place in most cities throughout Australia. An entire generation of Australians grew up with the image of banks as solid, trustworthy, dependable. No question was ever asked; all our savings went to the bank.

I also recall back in the 1970s when you had to kneel on both knees and have all your money with the bank before they would consider you for a loan. Now, despite glossy ads promising cheaper personal loans and even cheaper home loans, many, including the current baby-boomer-money-box generation, see the banks as self-serving and untrustworthy.

Angry customers, confused staff — what makes us feel such anger towards the banks? And what drives the banks to act more ruthlessly than ever? Such that would make even a prime minister in sheer frustration exclaim: 'I'd take a shotgun to them. Bang Bang!'

If banking has been intimidating and confusing for you, take the time to read this and 'know your enemy'.

I was concerned with the Xmas card on the notice board in the reception area of the Australian Consumers' Association's offices in Sydney. It read '*From The Combined Bank Robbers Association*' and it was signed: from the *Robbers of the NAB, the ANZ, Westpac*. The card was from a group of dissident customers of the banks. To suggest there was an angry and bitter tone radiating from the Xmas card, at a time when all men and women normally embrace each other with goodwill, is stating the obvious.

I had interviewed a number of 'victims' from these groups during the course of producing this book, and I was disturbed when I picked up a newsletter put out by one of the groups. In it was the caption which read as follows:

> 'How do tell when a bank manager is lying?
> You can see his lips moving.'

But recently, as a finance journalist, I have looked more closely at the banking system and how it affects most of us. I have come to the joyful conclusion that although there is an almost universal belief that what the banks say and do is cast in stone, this is very wrong!

Still, there are bitter people everywhere. And who can blame them? Banks report billion dollar profits at the same time as customers are hit with indiscriminate fee increases and often hidden costs. It gets up peoples' noses that a leading bank, the Colonial State Bank, for example, has the gall to advertise — prominently — one of its lending rates at 6.87 per cent. Gall, because that's not the rate you and I will actually pay. What you and I *actually* pay is 2.4 per cent more than this rate, after adding what the bank calls a 'customer margin'. Why can't they advertise the (higher) real rate?

And, in a classic case of 'do you want the good news or the bad news?', the Commonwealth Bank on the same day late last year placed two display ads in the papers: one saying '*Good news …*' detailing a 0.6 per cent fall in interest rates charged on various credit cards. The other ad '*News about Home Loans …*' detailing an *increase* in various fees charged on loans.

Or take the case of St George Bank that recently advertised: '*An important announcement: Our cash management rate is now up to 6.45% p.a.*' In small print (about one-quarter scale!) was a note: 'available to amounts of $100 000 or more.' The rate for smaller amounts, for example $5000, was 3.5 per cent.

Nearly half the 'come in sucker' rate. We are constantly treated like lambs to the slaughter!

The thing that struck me during my 15 years as a stockbroker and personal investment adviser was the number of times people complained to me about their bank. It was almost as if they needed someone to talk to. A financial confessional. And mostly it seemed to come from a feeling of powerlessness and helplessness. People complained about mistakes, about overcharging, about inflexibility, about indecipherable statements. My connection with these people became almost like the doctor–patient: 'Hello, how's your pain in the bank?'

The fact is that most of us feel ripped off by our banks. Don't you? Banks are in the business of making money. And they make the most money when they borrow at the lowest possible interest rate — from you and I — and lend it out at the highest possible rate which strikes most of us as very unfair. But for many, the straw that has broken the camel's back is that the banks are now cashing in on us by charging exorbitant and barely justifiable charges and fees, some of which have risen 200 per cent over the past year alone.

We feel captive and helpless. But, banks are fallible and can be beaten.

Competition has opened them up to a free market. Just like the sales assistant who sells you shoes down the street — banks need customers; they want to steal you away from the next shop; they will make deals with the wily shopper. For those who naturally barter and bargain when they shop this is easy. The rest of us can learn.

It helps for consumers to understand the nature of the beast and why it is fallible and open to negotiations. Banks are still reeling from the idiotic mistakes they made in the 1980s. During my time as a stockbroker I saw Westpac go on a lending binge and nearly go to the wall. For a while they pulled up the shutters — lending to virtually no one. Now, with a new management team they are aggressively seeking new business.

Knowing the psychology of the banks you are dealing with, their histories, philosophies and weaknesses, is as valuable a negotiating tool as knowing that the car yard down the street is going bust and the owner will do anything to get your business. You can and should exploit this knowledge.

And in the vein of 'knowledge is power' your second greatest negotiating skill is understanding what charges and fees are applied to your accounts: which are necessary, which are not and how you can use the banking system to your advantage.

The fear and intimidation we feel about banks and bank managers has to stop. We have to wrestle back control in this war of David versus Goliath. The battle cry is 'Know your enemy' and that is why I am writing this book. Learning from the common mistakes of some and the brilliant strategies of others we can win the war.

This book will guide you through the mazes of the banking world and give simple 'ready-to-wear' steps to take control of your own finances. A 'how to' in beating the banks and in profiting from it. Not just by saving on bank charges but also by creating real profit opportunities.

We can all learn how to beat the banks at their own game and how to end the financial tyranny were living under.

One thing has always bothered me. The banks enjoy and have enjoyed a virtual monopoly in the supply of credit — that is, loans — but have no fiduciary responsibility to the general community. In other words, the banks have a privileged position but they don't have to look after us. Their sole legal responsibility is to increase their returns to shareholders. That is to make more and more profits.

Bank profits get bigger and for too long now we have stood in queues that are far too long. At last there is some real competition between banks and non-banks, and we can now take one look at the queue and go elsewhere.

And, to take the metaphor further, if the queues get longer, ditch your bank account and buy some bank shares! When we all start moving out of the queues and into action, the big banks might finally get the message.

It was tapping into the ground swell of public outcry and the inherent injustice in the system that prompted this book. One of the great advantages of having been a stockbroker and a finance writer is being able to learn from and pick the brains of successful people. Now you have the opportunity to share in this wealth of experience.

Disclaimer

The contents of this book represent the opinions of the author and others. Because they are only opinions, readers should ensure that they seek independent advice before making any investment or borrowing decisions.

The rates quoted in the book were correct at the time of writing. In many cases they will have changed. Accordingly readers should make their own enquiries concerning current investment or borrowing terms.

Chapter 1

Banks don't do these sorts of things ... do they?

'Good morning, this is A speaking. How may I help you?'

'Good morning. I'd like a balance on my account.'

'Yes, madam, would you mind waiting a moment, and one of our transaction-account customer service personnel will assist you.'

A minute or so later, chirpy A the bank teller connected again: 'I'm sorry to keep you, but they shouldn't be much longer, would you care to hold on a moment or two longer?'

A 'moment or two' came and went. A, chirpy as ever, connected once again: 'I'm sorry to keep you, how may I help you?'

'Yes, I'm the one who wants an account balance, remember?'

'Oh, yes, madam, I'm sorry, I'll connect you right away. J will attend to your inquiry.'

'This is J speaking, how may I help you?'

'I'd like a balance on my account, please; my name is Jo-Anne Baker and my account number is —— .'

'Yes, madam, may I have your date of birth.'

'Date of birth? Why on earth do you want my date of birth?'

'Our new security arrangements now require us to verify all customer enquires that come over the phone.'

After submitting, Jo-Anne was finally given her account balance: a credit balance of $1900.

Jo-Anne, a successful business person and operator of a small mail order and retail business, had been dealing with banks for years, having pioneered the futon bed industry in Australia in the 1980s. This had been a particularly stressful week with suppliers' accounts needing to be settled.

As she got off the phone with J she felt physically ill. Believing she had $2900 in her account Jo-Anne had ordered goods to that amount. She panicked, calling her various debtors and pushing them to pay her immediately in a desperate attempt to raise the extra $1000 she thought she had.

Jo-Anne spent the whole day on the phone, putting off many other urgent matters and wasting a day's work to cover the shortfall in cash.

The following morning, with cheques in hand, she went to her bank. But before depositing them, she checked her account again with a different teller and was amazed to find her account with a credit balance of $2900.

Puzzled Jo-Anne spoke once again to J.

'You told me I had a credit balance of $1900 at 9.30 a.m. yesterday?'

'Yes, madam.' J checked the screen.

'But how do you explain the $2900 in my account?'

J was embarrassed. 'Ummm, it appears you had a $2900 credit balance yesterday ...'

'But you told me it was $1900, how could you make such a mistake? You even asked me the date of my birth.
I went into a complete state of panic because of you.'

'I'm sorry madam,' J replied. 'By the way, can I give you a brochure of our latest all-in-one-fee-free-wealth-optimiser account?'

This *mistake* really happened but Jo-Anne Baker has asked us not to name the bank or the teller. Another typical bank mistake was experienced by Joe N.

He accepted that his mortgage repayments based on a 9.5 per cent standard variable loan were correct. Three years later, when he went to switch to a cheaper lender, he found that he had been overcharged by $9 a month. This would have gone on for 25 years if unchecked.

Not all bank victims' gripes are about mistakes. Most, in fact, arise from being abused by the *system*. Consider, for example, this extract from a complaint letter published by the *Australian Financial Review* late last year:

> I know I'm just a mug punter, but I'm really baffled at how banks work. Why does it take five working days for cheques paid to me to be available for me to cash? As cheques I have paid out are debited immediately to my account. Signed Baffled Mug Punter.

Another Sydney complainant writing to Peter Burke for his book *You Can Bank on the Wails* tells of how he could not deposit a $70 000 superannuation payout from an insurance company into a term deposit with his bank until the cheque had been cleared! He presumably had to lose a week's interest first!

Or, consider the following snippet borrowed from an edition of the newsletter *Victims of the State Bank News*:

> Mr M runs a small business and in 1991 was forced to

> sell his property and repay the State Bank a substantial sum of money. Upon settlement of the property the proceeds were to be used to repay in full the company's overdraft and the account to be closed.
>
> The overdraft was repaid with a balance of 33 cents credit remaining on the statement. There were no other transactions initiated by Mr M. The bank failed to close the account.
>
> The bank's computer continued to accumulate charges, debt administration fees, interest and government charges. In just three short years the bank's computer, all by itself, managed to create over $18 000 of debt to the bank.

This is a book written for the long-suffering bank customer. Stories from disgruntled customers about their experiences with the heartless banks — whether from the young or aged, or the homemaker from the suburbs — are invaluable. These stories will provide the 'tips' on how to keep and make money.

Take the experience of a friend of mine 'N', who wanted to raise $30 000 for a home-based counselling practice. N owned her home outright and, apart from a few credit card obligations, was virtually debt free. She was told by her bank that they couldn't help, suggesting she'd be better off selling her $400 000 home to raise the money!

'It was so stupid and incompetent. I was made to feel worthless,' she said.

'Stupidity and incompetence' is one thing, but of even more concern is the widespread overcharging of interest. Former banker, Mr Kevin Nowland, has said some banks were over-charging to the tune of hundreds of millions a year by charging interest a day or two earlier than they should have, delaying interest rate cuts and triggering higher default rates through late payments.

Nowland, who had 14 years' experience in banking and

finance, was a former chief manager of a regional bank. He now operates The Interest Savers Pty Ltd which has developed a program called 'The Overdraft Saver' to check on overdrafts, term loans, commercial loans and deposit accounts.

'There is widespread and systematic action on the part of some of the banks to milk customers this way,' claims Kevin Nowland.

'Something's going on here and I don't know what it is,' somebody once said. And 'something' is very wrong when citizens — hundreds of them — form groups such as the Australians for Banking Justice and the like, in an attempt to combine resources and beat the banks.

Although a number of building society member action groups rose from the failure of several societies in the late 1980s, I have not come across Credit Union victims' groups or supermarket victims' groups, so I can only assume that the problems in banking are so widespread and the banks so intransigent that only through collective action can these *victims* gain sufficient clout to take on the banks.

Although the following paragraphs deal with some of the experiences of small business people, the principles outlined elsewhere in the book are relevant to everyone.

These *victims* speak not just in terms of overcharging, mistakes, but also in terms of 'corruption and abandonment of fiduciary duty' on the part of banks. Harsh words from bank customers so aggrieved as to go to any length to state their case.

Take Isaac Shields, for example, who has gone to the extent of setting up his own Internet site to 'show what the courts and banks are doing to us all'. The site displays court transcripts of his various battles against the banks through the court system, and provides a revealing chronology of bank power and domination.

Shields and his wife, who prior to his altercation with the

banks operated Shields Engineering on NSW's central coast, lost their business and home as a consequence of action taken by the bank.

'I now just want to embarrass the bastards,' Isaac said.

Marsha Wajnsztajn, the Sydney-based convenor of the Australians for Banking Justice, says the group has over 300 members, consisting mainly of bank customers from the small to medium-sized business community. Marsha, living in Sydney's eastern suburbs, has personally experienced what she calls a healthy dose of bank *rug-pulling*. The group's members had claims with the State Bank totalling over $100 million, representing losses alleged to be suffered as a result of bank action.

According to Marsha, hundreds of people have had their lives — businesses, homes, possessions — uprooted by what she claimed was a direct result of bank action.

Marsha believes the banks often know they are in the wrong. 'Why is it that when they do finally settle with a troublesome account they silence them with the threat of legal action if they should speak?'

Many of the other stories emanating from these groups can't be told at this point — to ensure any pending legal litigation is not jeopardised.

By the time I'd left the interview with Marsha Wajnsztajn, I was ready to fight.

One of the worst cases, according to Mr Eric Ellis, a member of the NSW state parliament, involved a couple who won an appeal against the State Bank — 'over the bank's misleading and deceptive conduct in obtaining a mortgage over their home before pulling the plug on a business loan' — but were still pursued by the bank.

Journalist Anne Lampe in an article titled 'Inquiry into bank disputes demanded' wrote of the case in the *Sydney Morning Herald* last June:

A day after receiving a demand to pay, the borrower, Mr George Patiadas, died of a heart attack. His widow continued to receive statements from the bank on which more than $190 000 of the bank's legal bills relating to the case are debited.

Mr Ellis highlighted an addendum to the bank's mortgage document which can trigger a whole range of penalties in the loan, resulting in a 'doubling of interest charges as penalties'. Another addendum states that the bank's estimate of the debt is protected from challenge as a condition of the contract contained in those hidden amendments.

Peeved by queues?

Most people associate banks not only with interest charges and fees but also with queues. Peter Burke tells this story in his book:

> Scene — CBA in a very busy shopping centre; time — 11.30 a.m. Thursday.
>
> There were about nine employees visible — all very relaxed. No senior staff were to be seen.
>
> Fifteen customers were patiently queuing and only one teller was operating. The bank employees chatted and sat at their desks looking less than fully occupied.
>
> At this moment I wished I had bought a cut lunch!
>
> Customer 14 stood it for about five minutes.
>
> Then he threw back his head and shouted, 'HELP!!!'
>
> Instant action!!
>
> Managers and accountants rushed out from previously hidden places. Three additional tellers started telling. People were being processed. The queue cleared in three minutes. Nuff said.
>
> Signed Peter S. from Wamberal

People in bank queues tend to hide their feelings fairly well (and, believe me, queues are getting longer due to branch closures and 'corporate downsizing'; that is, sackings). Banks seem to have less counter staff at lunchtimes when you need them. Banks have responded by kindly providing TV monitors to entertain people in the queues with in-house corporate propaganda or scenes from palm tree-ridden exotic islands to entice us to their travel products.

But it's not all gloom and doom: *this book is intended to offer hope and practical help*. The procedures outlined will help to simplify your banking, help you to make real savings and to get real returns from your money. *And then on to the real wealth-creating ideas.*

There are heroes too in the book — people from all walks of life, not just the rich and powerful, but ordinary people who saw the injustice of the system and stood up to it, and in doing so have used the system to their advantage and enriched their lives. Again, ordinary people — like Stephen Thaxter and John Symond.

A banker without a bank account

Stephen Thaxter's story is remarkable, not for its high stakes drama but for it's simplicity. It is all the more remarkable because this is the story about a banker without a bank account.

An associate director at Macquarie Investment Management, Stephen Thaxter, is putting what's called the investment basket plan into practice.

His entire income is placed into the bank's cash management trust, and periodic payments and direct debits are made from the trust as large bills, such as mortgage payments, fall due. Smaller, weekly-type bills are placed onto a credit card, taking full advantage of interest-free days.

'I do all my grocery shopping this way. My card issuer has a direct debit against my cash management trust account on a monthly basis. I don't have to remember to pay,' he says. This also saves on Eftpos-related fees which are charged each time they are used. A couple of times a month Stephen uses an American Express ATM to provide him with cash.

Although life without a cheque book would cause most of us to shrink with insecurity, Stephen Thaxter has, however, managed to streamline his banking to the point of paying virtually no bank fees. At the same time his money is earning full market interest rates rather than the 1 per cent or less most earn on transaction accounts. If anything is left over he uses it as a slush fund, which allows him to take advantage of investment opportunities.

'I noticed over the years that cash management trusts were traditionally used by investors for investment cash flows, but more and more people are using them for domestic-type cash flows*. 'Things are changing very quickly in banking.'

'The banks are greedy

John Symond, when speaking of the banks, is not short of punchy media-style grabs. Bank bashing may be a simpler way to describe it. 'The banks are greedy,' he adds. He is not short of stories about bank intimidation and power: John Symond, managing director of Aussie Home Loans, is a man who knows how to write his own history.

With only the scantest knowledge of his background John Symond has been anointed king by the masses for taking on the banks. So deeply embedded in our psyche is our fear and loathing of the banks that the relatively unknown Symond has become the darling of the media. He has been

*Later in the book we will look at exactly how a cash management trust can be used in this fashion.

projected in the David versus Goliath style — a champion of the public — for taking on and beating the biggest and most ruthless competitors in the country: the banks. In the space of five years, Aussie Home Loans has taken a huge slice of the home lending market away from the banks. A $200 million-a-month slice, representing nearly 10 per cent of the market.

What this means for the consumer is simple. Symond claims to have forced the banks to lower their rates to both existing and new borrowers by nearly two percentage points, achieving this by being the first on the market with a no frills type loan that undercuts existing bank lenders.

The effect of this on home borrowers has been twofold: new home buyers are now enjoying the benefits through cheaper and more flexible mortgages, and existing borrowers have been able to go back to their lenders and renegotiate their loans to meet the lower market rates.

Located in Parramatta, 30 minutes hard driving from the centre of Sydney and light years from the head offices of some of Australia's largest and most powerful banks, John Symond proudly takes me through to Aussie Home Loan's new boardroom. A room with a regular domestic dining table in the centre and, in a corner, a couple of armchairs around a coffee table. Both the room and its embellishments would be barely noticeable in the hallowed boardrooms of the big banks.

Yet, the mere mention of his name in those hallowed chambers would bring stony silence.

'This is what we're all about. A boardroom that accommodates just us — the owner-managers of Aussie,' said John. 'We will always remain independent. And independent of bank influence.'

John's vocal dislike of the banks is not played down. He has built his business around it, marketed it and won tens of thousands of customers. He has cleverly tapped into the anti-bank sentiment in the community by making beating the banks his credo.

In 1991 he was in the red to the tune of $3.5 million. Starting from a single office in Parramatta, his business today has over 500 employees, 50 000 customers, offices in most states and new business at the rate of over $200 million a month.

Time will yet tell whether this is sustainable or whether he will sell out or fade away. However, so far he has beaten the banks at their own game. One that the banks have regarded as their own sacred cow; one that generated more than $2.5 billion in pre-tax profits for the Big Four last year.

John knew the market well. 'Having pounded the streets. I knew what consumers wanted. In the first two years I went out there to people's living rooms, talking to them about their home loans.

'The average consumer took quotes from the bank for granted and more often than not they were socked for fees that they didn't expect. What they were quoted was an interest rate that was far too high. And more often than not they sat on their borrowings paying far too much for too many years, believing that they could not shift from their loans.

'The banks are squealing now because we're making them reveal all; often they've been giving misleading information.'

John's business formula was simple. Because he didn't carry the expensive branch structure of the banks, he would be able to source capital from the pool of institutional money and undercut the banks.

First, he had to convince and educate the public that mortgage rates change often and that there was flexibility available to them. Bank customers did not have to be locked in for 25 years. That they could change financier at any time.

Aussie Home Loans claims to have been the first to offer the 'honeymoon' mortgage with a 0.5 per cent discount for the first six months of payment. The press got hold of the story and elevated John Symond to hero status as the man who would 'keep the bastards honest'.

Aussie's product came out at a time when the banks were nursing wounds arising from the massive lending binge of the 1980s. Customers had been questioning why they should suffer to help the banks rectify their own bad decisions of the past. And more and more people were beginning to ask why banks continued to make billion-dollar profits.

'We did play on people's fear of having to go cap-in-hand to the bank for a loan. We went into people's homes and talked with them about how they should go about it. They are no longer getting stressed out, lining up to see the bank manager only to be told "no".'

Aussie Home Loans broke new ground. Never before had banking services been sold this way and the fear of banks challenged and broken down.

Aussie Home Loans took five months to lend out the first $50 million. At a time when the public loathed the banks more than ever before, it didn't take long for the avalanche to begin.

'I am a battler because I'd lost a fortune and I've had to battle to get where I am. I've now got a passionate desire to help the consumer.

'You work hard for your money. People deserve a better deal from their banks. They just want to be treated with a bit of dignity and respect and given a fair go. If they can't get it, they should move on.'

Chapter 2

The psychology of banks

Knowledge is power. It is unthinkable that, before any person buys a car, they not research the market to see what is available, who is the best dealer, which one is about to go out of business and is desperate for customers, which one provides the best back-up service and which dealer specialises in the car you most want to buy. There are different dealers to meet your different needs.

So too is it essential to have knowledge about your bank or banks in general, about the products they offer, about who specialises in which products, and about what motivates your bank and your bank manager. *This* will hold you in good stead when it comes to negotiating. Information is a powerful tool to be wielded at the negotiation table.

The presumption that we are all powerless against the banking system is incorrect. Banks are just businesses and, like any business, some are desperate for customers, others are smug and unyielding.

It pays to know the *culture* behind the various banks, their positioning in the market and their personalities. It pays to know the future moves on this *chessboard*. Who is from overseas and struggling to break into Australia to get a share of the consumer market. It pays to look behind the ads to know which banks are targeting which part of the market — St George, for example, tends to be the *family* bank and tries to be a leader in this area. It pays to ask which bank has just merged with another bank and wants a new bite of the cherry?

Consumers also have to realise that the advertisements promoting cheaper home loans on TV signal the same as a flashing light outside a hamburger joint. 'Come in and buy,' it says. Certain banks want your business. This was not always the case, but in this highly competitive environment it pays to know which one wants you the most. Which are more entrepreneurial? Which will waive fees to get you? Which live by rules and policies?

Knowledge can only help you. For instance, knowing if a bank is about to be swallowed up could be crucial to your negotiations.

Consumers have to be smart. Read the papers, watch the sign posts. Research the market and discover who's who in the zoo. You should also know the history behind the banks and how the events of the 1980s and what happens at the corporate level affects *you*. Remember, decisions made in the board room *do* filter down by way of memos to bank managers who are there to field your requests.

As a former stockbroker turned journalist I'd like to help you get to know the banks. What makes them tick, their weaknesses, their personalities. If banking has been intimidating and confusing for you, get to know 'the enemy'.

A quick overview

There are 50 banks operating in Australia. And just as each retail store has its own features, each bank, too, has its own 'personality'. Some banks are big, some small and agile. Some are specialists in one area or state, others elsewhere. Some are more efficient but arrogant. Others may be less efficient but eager to win business.

It may pay to use the more efficient bank for one purpose — running your transaction account, for example — and the one more eager to do business, for negotiating your home loan.

Throughout this chapter I will be giving you as many details as I can to help you understand the banking sector, and I will be offering tips on how you can use this information to your advantage. Here is a bird's eye view of who's who.

The Big Four

Westpac was the biggest of this group before experiencing huge losses at the end of the 1980s. Over the past five years it has undergone a massive restructure to recover lost ground. Recently it has consistently shown its ability to undercut the market in a number of key products. Very keen for business and potentially negotiable.

The ANZ has traditionally been commercially oriented and has often prided itself on its strong presence in the business centres of Sydney and Melbourne. It has a reputation for being smug (it made some of the most stupid blunders of all in the 1980s). It maintains, meanwhile, the largest overseas network of any Australian bank. Individual bank managers are known to have considerable discretion, so it is always a good contender for your business banking.

National Australia Bank, Australia's most profitable bank, did not make the mistakes that some of the others made in the

1980s and therefore it has a self-confidence and arrogance that may make it less flexible. The National Australia Bank remains the largest of the banks and has 28 per cent of all business customers. Possibly, therefore, it is the least accessible of the *Big Four* in terms of convenience of location and level of customer service for the person in the street.

The Commonwealth Bank was originally *'The people's bank'*. It was owned by the government it was there to look after the battler. However, in recent years it has become fully privatised (listed on the stock exchange) and is now struggling to shake off its image as *the elephant*. It is attempting to reposition itself as a highly competitive contender with a heavy advertising campaign.

The States and smaller, regional banks

Even though traditionally the majority of Australians tend to deal with one of the big four, be aware that around the country there are a myriad of other smaller, regional banks which have aggressively chased business.

According to the *Personal Investment Magazine*/Fujitsu 'Bank of the Year' annual survey, these smaller regionals are very service orientated, scoring the highest ticks for looking after customers' needs. They also appear to be very competitive in the home lending market.

St George Bank, for example, which mainly operates out of New South Wales, has established a good reputation. It is one of the few to offer *loyalty* discounts to long-standing customers. It very much plays up the image of being the family bank — good, wholesome and reliable — thus particularly competitive in the home-buyer sector of the market.

Other regionals such as Metway (QLD), Advance (NSW), Challenge (WA), and Bank of Melbourne (Vic.) have aggressively chased market share in home lending and small business lending. They appear keen to do deals.

The former State Bank of NSW, reeling from the shock of massive losses in the early 1990s and allegations of unconscionable conduct by groups of so-called *victims*, has now been acquired by the more conservative Colonial Mutual. A merged 'Colonial State Bank', wanting to redress this image, appears to be now more *out there*, offering competitive and sometimes innovative deals.

Meanwhile, so fierce is the bank competition for the mortgage market in Queensland, that prospective home buyers often don't even need a deposit to purchase a slice of new housing estates. Therefore, potential borrowers should definitely consider the local regional bank, which is bound to offer competitive rates in such a hot market.

Others

Macquarie Bank and Bankers Trust, two of the smaller, specialist banks, have consistently demonstrated high competence in the area of investment management. Investors take note.

US and Asian banks are moving in: Citibank has been active in rationalising its branch network and concentrating on high net worth individuals. Again this is useful for investors to consider.

Understanding bank managers

Its important to understand who you're dealing with and what motivates them. Many banks operate incentive schemes. Sometimes individual bank managers are locked into such schemes.

It is too simplistic to suggest that the managers we come into contact with are rewarded for the business they bring in. There is, however, little doubt that a bank culture emerged in the 1980s which saw bank managers on incentive programs related to the level of business they would *write*. That is, the amount of lending. There is little doubt that promotion opportunities were often directly linked to the size and volume of deals — particularly in the corporate area.

These days, after Westpac and ANZ in particular suffered massive bouts of financial indigestion from poor lending by some of these managers, there is a more sober environment.

It is still a fact, however, that memos flow from *upstairs* down to individual branch managers to do deals. These *deals* give a degree of flexibility to some individual branches to *match* deals against competing banks. This is particularly true for new business; that is, for business which is currently with another bank or is being touted around by a shop-wise consumer. Never underestimate the ability of you (the consumer) and they (the bank managers) to do deals.

Take care. For example, some bank staff may receive commissions if they sell you certain bank products. This is especially the case with a number of bank managed investment products such as unit share trusts. Be aware that the bank and/or bank manager may be in a position of conflict of interest here. Ask whether he or she does receive such a commission (under law this must be disclosed) and if so try for a cut! The manager can only say no, but at least you have put yourself in the power seat. Not the other way around.

It is, however, also true that some banks simply won't do deals. Others have very rigid structures where the loan approval process, for example, is inflexible. Others still have much higher *ratio* rules, for example, the ratio of repayments to salary which determines how much you can borrow, or the ratio of the loan against property value.

Remember that you are seldom dealing with an unassailable institution. You are not powerless. You do not need to go to the bank cap-in-hand begging for a loan. If you don't like the way you're being treated go elsewhere. You may find a completely different culture and attitude.

Don't be intimidated. There is much to be said about being armed with information. Not just in terms of what drives the bank and the bank manager, but also the corporate cultures behind the facades.

Who are the banks?

A brief history of the banking system will provide some valuable pointers on how to do business with them. Rather than being unassailable and the bastions of solidity banks exhibit some — if not all — of the human frailties. Each bank has a point of vulnerability. Just like David picked Goliath's weak spot, so too can you find a point which will be valuable for you in your own 'David and Goliath' struggle with the banks.

Banks are stupid

A finance journalist and her grandmother banked at the same branch — both with same surname and the first name initial. Their accounts were mixed up. For the year the finance journalist was overseas, she couldn't believe her luck as monthly deposits kept appearing while her poor grandmother, relying on rent income to survive, was unsure why her bank balance kept dwindling.

This same journalist wrote a story about a similar thing that happened at the corporate level. Two businessmen, each with the name Mr Leon Fink, had corporate accounts with the same bank. One was the late Leon Fink of Hoyts fame and the other was the Sydney property developer. What the bank did was inadvertently merge all the assets of the two Leon Finks by mistake, enabling both to borrow far in excess of allowable limits.

I will withhold the names of the banks, however they are among the Big Four.

There's little doubt that the 1980s were the breeding ground for some of the more dramatic excesses by the banks. It was a time when we saw bankers pursuing wheeler-dealers such as Elliott and Bond, and property developers with little substance but big plans. We saw Westpac nearly choke on its own excesses and ANZ lend hundreds of millions to a young man named Warwick Fairfax for a wildly ambitious plan to take over Fairfax. Young Warwick went on to send that venerable institution into receivership and help put ANZ into the red. And the list goes on …

As a partner in a medium-sized stockbroking firm in the 1980s I had considerable exposure to the banks. Business was good and stockbroking was good business for the banks. High activity with large demands on our finances meant large overdrafts and very substantial trust account deposits. Grist for the bank's mill.

I was one of five shareholder partners and to satisfy the bank's security arrangements for our business overdraft we had each pledged our family homes as collateral against the loan for the business. Not an entirely comfortable position for any of us, but one that would be familiar to virtually every small business person in the country. 'Bricks and mortar' was and remains the catchcry of every bank when it comes to security (not for the large fee paying Bonds and Skases, however).

Like many small businesses we were under-capitalised, and this meant very large overdrafts to fund the business, particularly when trading became brisk. And business was very brisk for most of 1986–87. So, like many firms we were dependent on the banks for their facilities to provide working capital.

And, like many businesses we were wooed by the banks.

What was meant to be a short-term modest loan became a long-term huge financial obligation.

One day early in May 1987 we were paid a visit by our bank manager — a Westpac CBD manager. We believed the bank wanted additional security for its loans and we attended the meeting with great trepidation.

To our amazement the manager outlined some commercial loan opportunities for investment. What he was doing was throwing money at us.

I recall talking of the possibility of investing in a commercial property. We became quite excited by this. Of course, I knew little about commercial property. But these were, after all, the heady 1980s and the banks played no small part in fuelling them.

While none of us took up the offer we remained nevertheless cavalier in our attitude to the availability of funding for the business. It was not until October 1987 that a new reality began to dawn. And it was not until much later — in my case, some years later, that I felt the full force of a bank moving in the opposite direction to my needs.

By the end of 1991 the bank was in reverse gear. Money which was freely available several years earlier had virtually dried up.

The billions written off (mainly in bad loans) by the banks between 1990 and 1993 were absorbed by a number of banks whose shareholders were forced to swallow a reduction in their share values. But it was the remaining creditworthy customers of banks who were forced to absorb much of these losses. *These customers, you and I, were slugged mercilessly for years afterwards.*

You can use this to your advantage by knowing which banks are competitive and which ones will do deals in order to make up for lost ground.

Westpac: a case study in stupidity — how to use it to your advantage

Because of the excesses described above, a new regime of managers took charge of Westpac and have been, for several years, redressing these through sharper and more aggressive trading.

During the 1991–92 financial year Westpac reported a $1.56 billion loss, one of the largest corporate losses ever reported by an Australian company. It's ill-fated romp into off-shore expansion and its binge on commercial property in the late 1980s brought the bank close to the financial wall. The bank was forced to write off more than a billion dollars in bad debts.

By their own admission, they'd made a mess of it. Patrick Handley, Westpac's chief financial officer, does not gloss over facts. 'We had very little financial discipline, and no financial management systems that were working. They were still investing heavily in commercial property when the rest of the world had worked out that was not the way.'

Big is better was the mantra. Big brings economies of scale and big provides the clout needed to tackle new non-bank competitors. *And big has always meant intimidation for the person on the street.*

Management upheaval and a string of director resignations shook Westpac to its very foundation, ensuring that the style of management which was prevalent through the 1980s was never too see daylight again.

In a climate of growth and market share domination Westpac had pulled out all stops. To some the prospect of an imminent bank collapse seemed like the just desserts.

Just how did a bank with total assets of $100 billion manage to get into this sort of strife? The answer lies essentially in the bank's relentless drive for business on virtually all fronts.

Early in the 1980s it began to occur to some bankers that raiders like Bond, Skase, Holmes à Court and Elliott represented tantalising profits. Raiders borrowed more money and paid more interest.

Dangerous lending practices crept in. Traditionally, Australian corporations had dealt with only one or two banks at a time. Now some corporations borrowed separately from several banks. Sometimes the banks were unaware of the corporation's exposure to each other. Some banks didn't even bother checking when amounts often totalled hundreds of millions. (Ironic, as when we borrow our minuscule amounts we have to tell them everything).

By the late 1980s this kind of lending had exploded. Rather than being prudent by spreading the risk, what the banks were doing, in fact, was aiding the creation of bloated corporations just waiting for an accident to happen.

Both the booms and busts of the 1980s were the greatest ever seen in this country. The busts among the corporates were nothing short of spectacular with the likes of Alan Bond, Christopher Skase and others losing billions of dollars of shareholders' and creditors' money.

The devastation was equally great among the financiers of their enterprises. Total write-offs and provisions by banks and financiers amounted to $28 billion. A huge amount — the equivalent of $3000 for each and every family in Australia.

Although the then Treasurer Paul Keating championed the cause of deregulation (a freeing up of the banking industry to competition from new players: local insurance companies, overseas banks etc.), preaching that competition would bring lower interest rates and better conditions for consumers from the banks, the banks instead competed by throwing money at corporate cowboys, many of whom were already insolvent.

According to Trevor Sykes, who wrote about these entrepreneurs in his book *The Bold Riders*, the key factor behind the crashes of the late 1980s was the 'prostitution of the banking system. The breakdown of the Australian banking system was both financial and moral.' Billions were lost in unsound lending by the banks, which are normally perceived as the 'guardians of the conservative monetary faith'.

One senior executive from Westpac recalled that around 1983 every corporate account manager in Westpac attended a three-week course on *relationship management* as it was called. 'The course was aimed at how you should go out and sell yourself.'

Perhaps worse, the banks structured staff incentives poorly. 'We had material rewards for business that gave very little focus on the quality of the credit.' This practice, common in the banking industry, meant bank officers were rewarded in proportion to the size of the deals. As the prime goal of each bank was to hold or increase market share, the main quality sought in bank chief executives was aggression.

Banking in the 1980s in Australia degenerated into a mad scramble to lend more and to maintain market share. Banks and governments were nearly pulled under as a consequence, and bank customers, who had nothing to do with these practices, became the victims.

In the 1990s consumers — including *you* — can derive some real benefits after years of being slugged for the banks' excesses. Westpac, as the case in point, was forced to restructure.

Whole layers of managers were sacked, hundreds of staff retrenched, branches closed and extensive staff retraining programs carried out. The consequence being a leaner and meaner competitor. Therefore, for the average consumer this provides an opportunity to get a competitive deal.

The 1990s: more of the same

NSW has the former state-owned State Bank as an example of a bank which had its own share of inept trading — particularly in the area of lending to small business. And, so inept was this regional bank that many former customers formed themselves into a *victims* group in an attempt to recover losses caused by the bank's actions.

The State Bank of NSW has now been taken over by Colonial Mutual and renamed the Colonial State Bank. It is keen to present a better image. What this means is that the combination of a new broom and past mistakes can present opportunities for consumers. Already the Colonial State Bank has shown itself to be a marketer of innovative banking products.

This recent merger is an illustration of where you, the consumer, might look either nationally or in your own state for opportunities. To keep abreast of what is going on, and how to capitalise on this you should regularly browse the pages of your local newspaper. Opportunities come in many forms, including fee-free home loans as an inducement to new customers. Always keep your eyes and ears open — 1997 will see a slew of new incentive schemes by the banks.

Banks are inefficient

We all end up paying for the banks' inefficiencies. Often the mundane aspects of banking: incorrect bank statements and lengthy waits on phone services are indicative of inefficiencies. We pay for them in the form of higher fees and charges and higher interest rates on loans. Now, in a mad scramble to regain efficiency the banks are closing branches at a rapid rate.

Knowing which banks are efficient or inefficient can be valuable because you may be able to get fee discounts or better service as a result of efficiency.

The problem for most consumers is that the big banks are lumbered with hugely inefficient branch structures and, more often that not, move as a thundering herd, all raising fees and charges in unison. You need to look out for the more deft operator, one who is capable of passing on efficiencies in the form of genuine lower costs to you, the consumer.

State and regional banks, because of their size, can sometimes (but not always) be slicker operators. For example, Bank of Melbourne has a good reputation in business banking, and Metway has a good reputation for offering competitive credit card rates. Advance is said to be good at service.

Many analysts believe that St George in NSW is an efficient operator and can afford to pass the monetary benefits of good management practices to the consumer. For instance, in the mortgage market St George has consistently passed on the benefit of cuts in official interest rates quicker than other banks. The benefits for you, the consumer, while not huge, are, nevertheless, real.

Of the Big Four, National Australia Bank seems to be one of the more efficient; however, because it is one of the most successful banks in this country, it tends to be more arrogant and less likely to pass on gains to the consumer.

Although banks are always bleating about how they are making great leaps in productivity and efficiency in order to deliver better deals to consumers, the truth is that they fall a long way short of what we are being led to believe.

Why are our banks so inefficient?

International consulting firm McKinseys pointed out last year that there is evidence that labour productivity at Australian banks is a mere 60 per cent of that in North America. Even the best local banks badly lag behind international best practice. Bank managements have proven mostly not up to the task of slashing cost structures.

In its November 1996 bulletin, the Reserve Bank said that while bank branches were being parred back by various banks as an efficiency measure, Australia still had more bank branches than countries with similar nationwide banking systems such as the United Kingdom or Canada.

What this means is that the banks carry enormous and unnecessary overheads and that these costs are incorporated in our fees and charges. In the home loan market, for example, the Reserve Bank estimates that the banks could slash their standard variable mortgage rates by another 0.75 per cent.

Yes, it's great to have our local bank conveniently located, but the reality is that it costs.

A banker I spoke to who preferred to remain anonymous suggested that the profit motive always preceded customer interest. 'I was amazed to find the company downsizing its human resources function. At a time of rapid changes, both at a company and an industry level, you would expect a greater commitment to training, not less.

'There is very poor morale out there. It will inevitably lead to inefficiency and poor customer service.'

In terms of efficiency measures we certainly see evidence in the form of branch closures and *downsizing* but these are not improvements that consumers can see and feel.

Criticisms of bank systems and practices abound. In its submission to the recent Wallis inquiry, the Consumer Credit Legal Centre of Sydney claims that the banks were effectively 'a generation behind in developing appropriate documents, training and computerisation, and procedures for the credit market of the 1990s.'

You should keep abreast of inefficiencies at your own bank and move to a more efficient bank. Also, look for non-bank operators such as credit unions and insurance companies. They do not carry the heavy burden of inefficient and expensive branch networks

Banks are unfair

This is not news. Don't presume the banks will always do the right thing by you. We're not talking about grand scale things here, but you need to:

- Check bank statements for accuracy.
- Check statements for possible fees introduced by stealth.
- Check interest charged and credited for accuracy.
- Check notices for announcements of new fees and other undesirables.
- Always be prepared to phone other banks or financial institutions for a comparison of bank fees and charges.

Know these facts:

I don't know of any other industry where companies are able to transfer moneys out of your account without first either sending you a bill or at least seeking permission. Or, where they can make changes in charges without notifying their customers beforehand. This position of power, domination and control has always been the way of the banks.

Banks are in the business of making money and the basis of them making money lies in their *borrowing* money from their customers — us — at the cheapest possible rate, and lending it back to borrowers at the highest possible rate. Banks borrow from their customers by offering interest rates for their deposits, savings accounts, cheque accounts and term deposits. They also buy from the professional money market, bank bills and other negotiable securities at a low rate and lend them out at a higher rate.

Clearly banks will attempt to minimise the cost of these borrowings to maximise the profits generated. And profits generated by the banks are awesome.

Banks are private enterprises and exist solely for the benefit of shareholders. And despite a monopoly control of credit in this country, the banks are not in the business of looking after us.

It should come as no surprise to anyone, therefore, that we always seem to receive less in interest in our savings accounts than we pay on our loan accounts. This is commonly referred to in banking circles as the *spread*, and it is this spread on the various businesses of the banks that determines how much profit they generate.

We need to realise that we are on the opposing side to the bank. That's fair enough — provided everyone is playing fair.

Rather than big profits, what grates most people is that banks seem to levy fees and charges on us wherever possible — often by unfair means or by stealth. It is just one area that you should watch closely.

Banks are sneaky

Chapter 3 of the book will show where banks slug you. Apart from the obvious — for reasons of profit — it's also useful to know why. This will arm you with the knowledge that banks don't always act in a straight fashion. Knowing this may give you that extra determination to beat them.

The banks have introduced fees by stealth. Last year Westpac, for example, announced a reduction in its home loan rates. It then wrote to customers advising them that they would have to pay a monthly fee. This fee was to apply to all customers even though it was pointed out to the bank that some of its earlier promotional material had promised that there would be no fees.

Back in the 1980s the banks had rapidly introduced electronic funds transfer systems and networks of ATMs to increase efficiencies. Unfortunately for the banks, most of the people who used the machines were young and made frequent use of ATMs to withdraw small amounts of cash but seldom to deposit it.

The banks were discovering that consumer behaviour could not be as neatly predicted as they had hoped. The discovery by the banks that they had misjudged the market for electronic banking led to a somewhat desperate search to find someone to pay for that misjudgment.

The patsy was to be the small depositor. Even as recently as last year, the Australian Consumers' Association assessed the major banks' fee structures, reporting in their Autumn 1996 issue under the headline that 'Basically, one hand giveth ... the other taketh away'. The assessment went along the following lines:

'While some account-keeping fees have gone, the transaction fee rises, in particular for electronic banking, have led to dramatic increases in banking costs. In some cases the net cost to consumers increased by hundreds of percentage points, while for the typical family — medium balance — resulted in additional costs having to be borne.'

But it's not just fees that the banks are chasing. Chris Gosselin, managing director of Market Faxts, an information service monitoring bank interest rates, stated:

'Bank margins got hit very hard on one of their biggest profit generators: home lending.

'In the period August 1994 to June 1996, bank margins were slashed from 4 per cent to 2.25 per cent. All due to non-bank competition.

As far as the banks were concerned this had to be recovered. That's what they're doing all the time with fees. Now they're trying to squeeze more margin out of their credit card and commercial lending operations.'

We have a long way to go before we have a level playing field. But at the very least we can know the facts.

Banks make too much profit

Australian banks do make too much profit. You'll see why this is so in the following paragraphs. But there are still banks out there looking to improve their position in the market. The National Australia Bank does not make $2 billion a year profit from being generous to its customers, so there is a case for you, the consumer, to take a good look outside the billion dollar profit earners to the smaller, regional banks. They could offer better deals.

Bank profits. A *billion* dollars rolls off the tongue quite easily. That's the magnitude of profits that some banks are generating. The Big Four earned a total of $5 billion for 1996. That's $5 billion generated from borrowing from our accounts and lending it back to us for our mortgages, our cars and our businesses. Profits of the banking industry as a whole are the profit powerhouse of Australian industry, *and more profitable than banks anywhere else in the world.**

Given the size of these profits, particularly from the Big Four, banks are always going to have real trouble winning back the hearts and minds of us ordinary citizens. Increased fees, for example, while rationally argued for by the banks leave few of us with any real doubt about their real motivation: no more than a basic instinct to protect bottom line profits. And, while this is good for shareholders and executives on incentive schemes, it is does nothing but take money out of our pockets.

So, how much profit is enough? And why in an age of computerisation aren't bank costs going down at a faster rate than their fee increases?

---

*For the world's 200 largest banks, as measured by shareholders' funds, the average return on equity for 1995 was 8.5 per cent — according to a survey by *Euromoney*. This compares with an average of 16 per cent for the Big Four.

The Reserve Bank, meanwhile, also believes that bank (profit) margins are not internationally competitive. In one of its bulletins (September 1996) the Bank looked at the spread between the price charged for a standard mortgage by banks in Canada, New Zealand and the United Kingdom. The cost of providing the funds for those loans, was 1.5 per cent. In Australia, the comparable figure was 50 per cent higher at 2.25 per cent. In simple terms, what this means is that we're still paying far too much interest on our loans.

Never reticent to present their case, banks argue that consumers are better off than ever and that bank profits are not excessive. Mr Kevin Broadribb, media spokesperson for the Australian Bankers Association claims that bank bashing is always fair game, but the *truth* is that banks only make *average* profits. 'They are in fact well within the range of what shareholders would expect from their investments. In terms of returns, the big four banks return between 14 and 17 per cent on shareholder equity.' (Recent results, in fact, show a return on equity of over 18 per cent in the case of ANZ.)

Imagine yourself as an investor in a business. What would you expect in return for your money, remembering that a risk-free investment such as a term deposit in the bank would return around 6 per cent? Is it not unreasonable to expect an investment in business to be considerably higher? By way of comparison, BHP, Australia's largest public company, shows a return on shareholders' equity of 15 per cent.

The argument is not so much a case of whether banks are making *excessive* profits but whether they running their businesses efficiently or making us pay for their inefficiencies. Banks, after all, are granted licences — some say to print money — and operate in a very protected environment which is much less competitive than many other businesses, for example, BHP's.

Sorry. There are no obvious ways of beating such greed. It makes me very angry that banks are so ruthless for profit. My fantasy is that one day enough people will withdraw their money from inside the banks and reinvest it elsewhere — including bank shares! Then we may see a change to the system. But I'm not holding my breath.

Banks milking the customers

Why do Australians continue to keep such a large proportion of their money in non-interest paying and low interest deposits? Pensioners, for example, have traditionally left most of their savings in the bank. Usually for security reasons.

It is understandable that many of our senior citizens need the security of money in the bank. But there really is no excuse for the rest of us to leave money in low interest-bearing accounts. Yet, many people are passive. And passivity costs. Take note: you can always try to improve on your bank's current offer by shopping around.

Banks do receive a very large percentage of their money free or at very low rates of interest. There are several reasons for this. Apart from pensioners, who are a special case (pensioners, who have different needs to those with growing families or debts, often have large and static deposits), many people still behave as if banks are the only option for their savings, failing to adjust to a changed banking economy.

That is to say, many consumers still act as if higher rates on deposits were available only to the rich! If there was ever a behaviour counter to getting richer this much surely be one. You need to be on your toes — banks seldom act in your best interest.

Study, for example, the behaviour of the banks in the light of changes in interest rates: over the period June 1994 to June 1996 the 90-day bank bill rate (the rate which determines what banks charge) increased by 2.74 per cent.

Because of intense competition in the home lending market the banks only upped the variable mortgage rate by 1 per cent.

Small businesses were slugged an extra 1.95 per cent (at least) via the small business variable rate, but ordinary depositors (who have never really seen competitive rates offered to them) saw their rates lifted a mere 1.5 per cent.

This kind of behaviour has prompted the Federal Government to speak up. Late last year the Treasurer, Mr Peter Costello, attacked the banks in Parliament for taking twice as long to slice rates for customers (after the interest rate easings) as they had taken when lifting retail rates after official increases in 1994.

So, once again the small bank depositor gets slugged. He or she misses out on market movements. The depositor's loss is the bank's gain. I advise all consumers to do a quick phone around to find out what deposit rates the different banks and non-banks (i.e. credit unions) are offering. Getting competitive quotes is an essential part of taking control.

'Banks are bastards'

I can vividly recall this headline in *The Bulletin* for its 2 May 1989 edition. It effectively caught the mood of the day. The complaint was that the banks had hurt the ordinary battler to pay for their own indiscretions.

Although this is a headline of a number of years ago it still sums up a prevailing sentiment in the community. Keep this in mind when next you think of such values as *loyalty* and *security*.

I've also borrowed from John Edward's 1996 biography of Paul Keating to bring you a chillingly amusing exchange between Keating and one of his closest advisers prior to the 1993 election. Keating said: 'The banks buggered us. You hear it perpetually — the banks won't lend.'

The then governor of the Reserve Bank replies: 'We still hear reports of them seeking 15 per cent profit after tax.'

To which Keating is reported as saying: 'I'd take a shotgun to them — bang, bang. I'll get them when I'm more powerful.'

Many of us who grew up in the era of taking the money box to the friendly bank and feeling all warm and fuzzy, live with a contradiction. We still remember when their mortgage rates hit 17 per cent several years ago. The rise in interest rates came at the same time as banks announced that their half-yearly profits had risen by over 50 per cent. Householders were hurting but banks were adding to their *indecent* profits with high margins and additional bank charges.

Complaints about bank service also mounted as banks decreased their counter staff in an attempt to prune costs. Even the popularity of the ATMs was seen as an indictment of bank service. More recently, Susan Brooks, a former Australian Banking Industry Ombudsman, said in her 1995 annual report that 'Few Australians would disagree that ... a negative view of the banking industry has developed.'

If anything this is on the increase. In the three years to the end of 1995 the office of the Ombudsman had received over 100 000 telephone complaints covering a wide range of issues, most of which revolved around the customer believing they had been financially disadvantaged as a result of bank action (or lack of action).

But this is only the tip of the iceberg. Many bank customers do not bother or do not know what remedies are available to them. Then there are those that fall outside the Ombudsman's net. Small business people, for example. I have already referred to the hundreds of members of victims groups — desperate people tied together for a common purpose.

I've heard former victims speak of *beating the banks*. One person said bitterly: 'Yes I have beaten the banks because I only lost half of my possessions.' People spoke of intimidation and the banks' strategy of fighting through the full length of the court system in order to drain their opponent's resources.

Former banker Kevin Nowland believes that the banks are not the innocents they claim. Knowles, who has developed a software program for allowing consumers to check interest rates levied and credited to accounts, believes that there is a widespread problem.

> We have found that banks overcharge in very many accounts. Over a 54-month period we tested a number of accounts and found that overcharging occurred in 29 of these months.
>
> In another instance of incorrect calculation we found that an insurance broking firm had been underpaid interest of $60 000!
>
> That company operated a number of trust accounts which had varying balances. What the bank did was apply a flat rate of interest — the lowest — across all the accounts rather than higher rates for higher balances.
>
> When we went to them, their comment was: You're quite right; we're surprised it's taken you so long to find out.

Getting a better deal

Banking is changing. Gone are the days of the cup of tea with the bank manager. Now a mobile lender comes into the living room to discuss a home loan. No longer the familiar friendly face at the local bank. Now an ATM or a phone.

You do need to change habits and *get with the times*. It is to your advantage. It will help you regain control and get back in the driver's seat. If you fail to change you will inevitably be paying too much and certainly wasting time in bank queues that are far too long.

It's a peculiar phenomenon, these banking habits which plague most Australians. People will shop around for the best value on, say, a washing machine, but they have been reluctant to shop around for better banking deals (with the home loan market a notable exception) that can save them tens of thousands of dollars in some instances.

What's worse, until recently many consumers have not been able to compare the full costs of loans because they have not been aware of such items as exit fees and other 'hidden' charges. Even with the new Consumer Credit Code customers may have to search the small print, a task usually avoided by most of us.

Now there is more information readily available on what's going on behind the mighty bank walls. Consumers can see exposés on national current affairs programs or read about the banks in their newspapers. And banks are now obliged to inform consumers about what is really happening behind their closed doors when it comes to fees and charges. All this gives us the freedom to act, to take control and to vote with our feet.

But still, old habits die hard. Market studies have shown that adult customers still resist changing their finance institution, for it is seen in terms of a lasting loyal relationship rather than a business arrangement. In Chapter 5 we will look at this question of bank loyalty and assess its real worth.

According to well-known psychologist, Hugh Mackay, while mobile lenders and ATMs have given consumers back some control, he also noted that 'there is some anxiety and insecurity for the customer because he or she must now take charge'.

Many customers still feel vulnerable around banks, for example, when applying for a loan. The customer once had to go cap in hand, and a loan was once something for which the customer had to be grateful. He or she had to show not only an ability to repay but also evidence of loyalty to the bank. The other side of the coin was the feeling that the banker was a trusted financial adviser who knew customers personally and made sure that they did not get in over their heads.

'Now there is a sense out there that banks have moved from a position of support to one of: *they're out to get us*.

'Underlying is a feeling of hostility,' said Hugh McKay.

We need to distance ourselves from bank intimidation, from being so emotional about this unhealthy paternalistic relationship and to stop feeling like the banks are our adoring big brothers or fathers, who are always fair and always know best.

In essence, we have to grow up and take control. We have to shrug off the illusion that we are being cared for and to remind ourselves: *Banks are uncaring. They are also extremely fallible*. But you do need to have a preparedness to act. It is no use being rendered passive by rage and frustration. Let the anger be your fuel.

Psychology in action: the home loan market

On the whole, banks are slowly losing their aura of invincibility and nowhere is this more evident than in the battleground being fought in our own backyards. Consider the case of Anne and Westpac as a simple illustration of the value of *knowing* a particular bank's psychology.

Anne wanted to trade up her home. She planned to sell her small bed-sitter for a larger two-bedroom town house, so she needed to refinance.

'I went to my bank, the Advance, and asked whether they could change over the mortgage to the new property. They said I would have to re-apply, including resubmitting tax returns to show my last year's income. I was shocked and annoyed.

'I knew Westpac were hungry for business. This was three

years ago and they had come out of a massive restructure. I went to them and they jumped at the deal.

'They were so excited I wanted to leave Advance; they didn't want to see anything — just the property.

'I recall speaking with a senior executive at Advance Bank, telling him of my experience. He was very upset and angry.

'Bank managers hate losing customers to the opposition.

'Advance then went on to change some of their old rules. Unfortunately it was too late.'

Westpac, having turned its fortunes to a position of near market leadership from one of near disaster has become a more market-oriented bank. Its current position reflects its ability to respond quickly to competition. The concerted effort to deliver a better deal to customers — and enhance its own position — has also helped the bank recover from its difficulties in the early 1990s, when bad debts crippled its ability to move quickly.

The direct benefit for the consumer is the opportunity to secure competitive products. Moreover, customers on existing mortgages, armed with information, could negotiate better deals on their loans from the bank.

What fascinates in this titanic struggle between huge organisations competing for our mortgage and investment dollars is how a bank which was in many respects a basket case has thrust itself in front of the market as a bank which will *do deals*.

At a personal level, this *can* mean better deals, but what is really needed is for all of us to approach banking with the attitude: *don't be a victim, get organised — be informed.* And it's not just competition between banks that opens up opportunities for the watchful consumer. Non-banks are always an alternative.

In home lending, banking's most important product area, for example, price competition emerged in 1993 but did not really get going until 1995. Newcomers, such as John Symond's Aussie Home Loans, took the fight to the banks with genuine cheaper loans and very quick sales service. The banks responded and what we have seen since 1995 is real sustainable competition for our mortgage dollar.

While the mortgage market is a notable exception even there it took a non-bank institution, namely Aussie Home Loans, to shake cheaper loans out of them. Banks fight to the death for profit margin.

John Symond of Aussie Home Loans says: 'It's sheer competitive forces that are pushing interest rates to where they are. We've forced the banks to move. They're not doing it for the love of the customer; it's because they are losing them in droves.'

Up to 1994 the banks had over 90 per cent of the home loan market. Now it's 80 per cent. By the end of 1997 it could be down to 70 per cent. Money *is* moving away from the banks. For you, the consumer, it puts you in the power seat to know how banks behave when their 'turf' is threatened.

Summing up

One thing is certain, we will have to remain on our toes. Banks will get bigger and more powerful. More powerful banks drive harder bargains. And the trends in place will roll on relentlessly leaving many consumers behind — caught in a time warp.

Apart from mergers, the strongest trends in banking have been the emergence of electronic banking, branch closures and the new breed of non-banks: mortgage originators such as Aussies Home Loans and RAMS (the trade mark of RAMS Mortgage Corporation), and the thrust by credit unions into personal loans.

Now (as I will discuss later in the book) for the first time banks are facing real competition in the credit card market too.

Consumers armed with knowledge have the power to take on the banks on new fronts. Competition between the banks and the newer players will throw up opportunities for you, the consumer.

Failure to keep up with these changes will see you fall behind. As a case in point, look at the plight of small depositors — the majority of the population — who have gained least from the changes in the banking industry. Low as the interest paid on savings accounts is, the cost of servicing them has come to be regarded as an increasing burden by the Australian banks.

As the banks' priorities move away from them, it is likely that these customers will be offered lower basic levels of service. Facilities that used to attract no fees will increasingly be charged for. *This is more reason to take control of your finances and look at alternatives.*

With increased competition for your business comes a barrage of ads and glossy brochures. You, the consumer, will have to be alert to what is really being offered and whether it is the best product for you.

The spate of mergers and takeovers we saw last year in the banking industry will continue, creating even more powerful mega banks. It has been a notable feature of the banking industry that under the threat of competition banks tend to respond by merging with each other rather than standing alone to fight and offering real benefits: lower prices; higher rates; better service.

In an example of customers being left out in the cold, late last year the Bank of Melbourne, having purchased the Victorian banking assets of Challenge Bank, closed 15 of the 22 Challenge branches acquired. There is little doubt that this trend will continue. In this particular case, my guess is that the only the beneficiary will be the Bank of Melbourne and its shareholders.

Even the possibility of a bank merger between, say, a National Bank and Westpac or a National–ANZ marriage has been mooted. The attraction for National — being the larger — is obvious. And the motivation? Profit.

The benefit may be obvious to shareholders and executives of both banks, but the majority — the consumers — will have to wait a long time for real benefits to flow to them. Bank mergers generally fail to deliver long-term benefits to the community — mergers mean bank closures. A Westpac takeover, for example, could mean the loss of 500 branches according to some analysts.

But once again, bank closures can mean opportunities for the smart consumer. It forces you, the customer, to face up to the fact that the banks are moving away from servicing customers at their branches in the traditional way. *You need to adopt more contemporary banking habits.*

The Reserve Bank in a recent bulletin has stated that 'electronic banking services can, in part, substitute for bank branches'. In fact, the Bank noted that late last year the number of ATMs overtook the number of bank branches for the first time — exceeding 6507! There is little doubt that that electronic technology is becoming more widely accepted by consumers.

Smart consumers everywhere are not only physically staying away from bank branches in droves — choosing to use electronic and telephone means — but are switching to non-banks for their financial needs. This is smart because it gives back control to the customer.

Erica Goatly keeps several accounts, which she monitors closely and attends to regularly. But she finds she rarely needs to visit the bank. Instead, most of her banking is done over the phone or via the fax.

'It's been months since I've set foot inside a bank. As far as I'm concerned, my bank branch could be in London or North

Queensland. When I need to move money from one account to another or when I want to order statements or review deposits I use the telephone or fax.'

Holding several accounts with the ANZ, a cash management account with Potter Warburg and keeping on top of transactions in each account could be time consuming and inconvenient, particularly when Erica's central Sydney ANZ branch, where she has built a relationship with staff, is no longer easy to visit on a casual basis.

'Since I'm not in the city much now, it's a real problem getting to the branch. It takes time, you have to find somewhere to park — it is just a hassle.

'The relationship I have on the phone is warm and it's much better than I'd be likely to have with people locally. It's really an effective way of dealing.'

Operating by telephone actually helps Erica to find the most competitive interest rates. It is easier to contact other financial institutions to assess their rates than being in a bank and facing pressure to sign up at the first rate offered.

'I do a fair amount of negotiating on the interest rate payable, especially on the money I have in the ANZ cash trust. They contact me periodically to discuss reinvesting the income and they'll quote me an interest rate. I then ring around and see what others are paying. If I can find a better rate elsewhere, ANZ will have to match it to keep the business.

'It's a bit of a game. They'll offer to meet the rate difference half way because it'd cost both parties money to actually move funds across. It's amazing what a difference it can make.

'Times have changed because of electronic banking. You're no longer face-to-face and that means loyalty is not really a factor any more.

'I can move money from any one of my accounts: for example, from Potter Warburg to the ANZ account, or to my superannuation fund. I usually fax the instruction, then I have my own record of the transaction. Otherwise, I have a PIN number which I use for the ANZ business.'

Erica reckons she's saved thousands of dollars by maintaining a business-like approach to her banking business. She represents the new breed of bank consumer.

Not one to be intimidated by bank pressures, Erica has enriched her lifestyle by beating the banks.

'We pay a lot to have bank accounts. They are not doing us any favours by running them.'

Electronic banking has thrust the consumer into the control seat. Intimidation on the banks' own turf can be eliminated. The evidence that increasing numbers of Australians prefer banking with smaller banks and non-bank financial institutions — especially for their mortgages — should tell us that something very profound is happening out there. MLC Building Society, for example, now promotes itself as pioneering 'branchless banking'.

As far as credit cards, business lending and competitive interest on savings are concerned, there's a lot of room for more effective competition.

There's still much to learn to achieve a real victory over the banks. This book will equip you with what you need in this battle.

Chapter 3

Bank fees and charges: where they slug you

It's a simple proposition: if you do nothing you'll be paying too much in bank fees and charges! We'll detail the full range of fees and charges and how they affect you, and give you some simple tips on how to avoid them.

'People don't even bother complaining any more. It's just too annoying.' Peter Kell, senior policy officer from the Australian Consumers' Association, may well have been referring to the hundreds of ways banks annoy and irritate us — fees, errors and omissions, and indecipherable statements. He was, however, referring to a more profound and serious issue: the way banks present their various charges.

> 'I went to withdraw $10 from my 8-year-old daughter's account and found that instead of accumulating interest, the account had been closed because it had not been used for 12 months. I then found that four of the five savings accounts had been closed for the same reason. My 8-year-old lost 50 per

cent of her savings in charges and taxes. This is appalling; I am a single parent with five children to care for, and spare money for 'savings' is so hard to come by.'

Mrs C. D.

Consider the case of Debbie, who took out a home loan with Westpac after checking out a few banks on their rates and charges.

'The bank was very helpful — even doing the calculation of what it would cost if I borrowed from the other bank.

'I borrowed $110 000 over 25 years and was pleased with my $890 a month repayments.

'But then, less than 6 weeks after I negotiated my loan, I received a letter advising me that I was going to be charged $8 a month for a loan administration fee.

'I would not have taken the loan if they had told me. I feel betrayed and very angry about the whole thing.'

The sad letter above from Mrs C. D. appeared in *You Can Bank on the Wails*, a book by Peter Burke, citing more than a hundred cases of battles between banker and customer. But there are literally thousands of stories like this to tell about bank fees. People feel violated when they get hit with fees that they don't expect. After all, in the real world, we are all used to getting a bill or an account *before* we are hit. In the world of banking this is not the case.

Typical also, is the case of the pensioner who was charged $15 for forgetting to put his signature on a cheque. The bank debited this amount to his account as a *reference* fee. The bank could have referred this innocent omission to the pensioner by way of a phone call. Is such reasonable behaviour from one of the banks too much to ask?

Particularly irritating is the practice of charging you, the creditor, something like $9 when a cheque you deposit turns out to be a *dud*. If you are already paying an account fee why another hit? Sure, the banks shouldn't be the ones to wear the cost of dud credit, but there must be a better way rather than to slug the innocent customer — twice!

Some rebel against bank fees and charges in their own way. What, for instance, would make a young, professional woman in a busy suburban legal practice walk 40 minutes every week to her bank just to pick up a bundle of cash?

'Bank arrogance,' says Lee. After sacrificing her cheque book in a symbolic funeral pyre in protest against unheralded fees and charges, she now pays her bills in person and in cash.

Why wouldn't she just use a hole in the wall for her cash needs or a cheque book to pay her bills?

'I try to avoid the banks wherever possible. They won't get my money,' she said.

This angry customer is not alone and while her brand of protest will bring more satisfaction than profit, it is, nevertheless, her way of beating the banks. Above all, the problem is so extensive as to affect virtually every one of us.

'The problem is very deep rooted,' says Peter Kell from the Australian Consumers' Association. 'People coming into the bank with problems or complaints don't get any satisfaction. People don't even bother complaining any more. They just give up.'

Fees by stealth

According to Peter Kell, 'Fee increases by the banks are something the Australian Consumers' Association look at very closely.

'For too long we have heard the argument that banks must make the user pay. And that's just what they're now doing. Last year (1996), for instance, the proposed average hike in fees for the four major banks was:

- 65 per cent (for a typical young, single consumer)
- 223 per cent (for a family using the same account with two children) and
- 40 per cent (for a well off, single consumer).'

The Consumers' Association also calculates that the average transaction account balance, which holds $6770, can earn banks $186 a year, since banks pay consumers lower interest for deposits while the bank earns higher interest on lending.

'We must break down the myth that retail transaction accounts cost banks money, because in fact they can generate comfortable profits once interest is taken into account.'

A Prices Surveillance Authority inquiry concluded people should have a *right* to access banking. Early in 1996, in response to government and consumer pressure, banks expanded personal transaction account options, splitting the account into two types. Basic, or low-volume, accounts were designed to avoid charges for low-balance account holders who would deposit and withdraw regular amounts but use the account for little else. Higher volume accounts will be looked at in the section on transaction fees below.

Fees and charges: the direct hits

Before making suggestions on how to save on bank fees and charges let's list them. Later in the chapter we'll use the example of Sally and Roger to show how fees can be reduced. In Chapter 4 we'll proceed through the steps necessary to run virtually fee-free banking. But first, the three types of bank fees and charges:

- account-keeping fees
- transaction fees, and
- one-off fees.

Account-keeping fees are the regular variety of fees applied by banks each month when the minimum monthly balance falls below a certain amount (often $500). For personal transaction accounts fees range from zero to around $12 a month. Savings accounts attract a fee of between $2 to $5 a month from most banks.

Transaction fees are levied in a variety of ways. Many accounts have a set number of free transactions — these include writing and depositing cheques, ATM use, over-the-counter (OTC) bank use, Eftpos — per month after which you will be charged fees. Here, customers can expect to pay up to $1.50 for OTC withdrawals, while cheque withdrawal fees range from 45c to $1.25. Some banks won't charge these fees if you are over a certain balance. Lack of attention in an active account could result in fees in excess of $30 per month. One of the biggest fee traps is using other banks' ATMs. With very few exceptions, banks do not include use of other banks' ATMs in free transactions, and the going rate is between 75c and $1 per visit.

One-off fees are the hardest to contain; they can be quite elusive and are charged for items like overdrawing your account or buying a bank cheque. The list below shows the bewildering array of some of these charges. ***Almost every aspect of banking can incur some kind of cost.***

Most arise through lack of planning. One-off charges can be very steep. It's easy to forget this because such charges are incurred infrequently and details about them are harder to find. For example, if you accidentally bounce a cheque from your Westpac or NAB account, you'll face a fee of up to $35 — completely swamping any savings you may make on monthly account keeping fees!

Look out for charges on:

- ATM use
- bank cheques — purchase
- administration fees
- telegraphic transfers
- charges from overseas bank for telegraphic transfers
- new cheque books to be issued
- credit transfers to another bank — internal clearing
- credit transfers to another bank — by mail
- dormant accounts
- stopping payment on a cheque
- 'fast' clearance on a cheque
- stopping any drawing on the account
- restricting those who make drawings on the account
- accidentally overdrawn accounts
- periodic payment deductions — for another branch e.g. car payment
- periodic payment deductions — for another bank e.g. health fund
- dishonour fee outward cheques
- dishonour fee inward cheques
- dishonoured direct debits
- notification by telephone of dishonoured cheques
- replacement bank statements
- audit letters
- record searches (e.g. earlier cheque).

Fees to avoid

- dishonour fees — your payment
- dishonour fees — another person's payment
- payment or drawing by non-approved means

- fees and costs following a default.

These can be very costly.

Government taxes

Government also hits your transaction accounts. In many cases taxes may outweigh bank charges.

There are two types of tax:

- the Financial Institutions Duty (FID) and
- the Bank Accounts Debit Tax (now officially called the Debits Tax, but still known as BAD). Both are paid to state/territory governments.

FID is applied to any credit, that is, *deposit* made to an account — savings accounts, cheque accounts and credit cards except in Queensland. It applies a flat percentage of the deposit, which is 0.06 per cent in most states. This means that on a deposit of $1000 you will pay FID of 60 cents. This may not seem like much, but if your entire year's salary goes into your account FID can add up to a significant amount.

	NSW and VIC	QLD	WA	SA	TAS	NT	ACT
Cost per $100 deposit	6c	nil	6c	6.5c	6c	6c	10c

BAD is levied on all *withdrawals* from all accounts with a cheque facility, except in the ACT (exempt). It's based on a sliding scale that impacts relatively more on withdrawals of lesser amounts. BAD has a greater impact than FID on most customers. In NSW, SA and Victoria, for example, BAD tax is applied at the following rates:

Amount withdrawn	**Fee charged**
$1 to $99	$0.30
$100 to $499	$0.70
$500 to $4999	$1.50
$5000 to $9999	$3.00
More than $10 000	$4.00

A *typical* transaction account may have several withdrawals of $100 to $499 a month. It may also have the odd larger one — say one $1500 withdrawal several times a year. This would incur between $35 and $40 a year in BAD taxes.

Stephen, 16, had been saving for a mountain bike for two years. He understood how interest could compound and add value to his savings. With only $200 or so in his savings account he knew that interest would not be high. However, he was shocked to find that more than half the interest he had earned had been eaten up by government charges.

On average, customers who keep less than $500 in their account will lose 65 per cent of the interest earned by that account in FID. Where the account has a cheque facility, the cost of the debits tax can be many times greater than the amount of interest earned. When added to the deposits tax, you can soon see how taxes can erode a bank balance!

A few institutions will absorb the cost of FID and/or BAD on particular accounts, or for particular classes of customers, such as people with deeming accounts (pensioners' accounts; see Chapter 12).

The combination of FID and BAD serves as a disincentive to moving money between accounts and changing accounts — they impose costs on both the opening and closing of accounts. You will need to carefully assess the costs of moving accounts.

How to avoid the fee trap: too many eggs in too many baskets

Sally and Roger keep a number of accounts. Sally, who looks after the household accounts, doesn't know exactly how many. She and Roger married five years ago and decided it would be good for each of them to keep a personal savings account — 'a private nest egg; just for little luxuries — you know.'

Sally and Roger have their joint cheque account at the bank down the road. They also keep a savings account there, saving for that overseas trip or investment property. They've saved about $8000 so far.

Each of them have ATM access cards linked to the cheque account. In addition, each have credit cards from their single days. They also have one in joint names. They have opened savings accounts for each of their two children — with only a few dollars in each. 'We might have to take school fees from them if they save too much,' laughs Sally.

Sally and Roger have a mortgage at another bank. 'We shopped around and found one of the smaller banks. They gave us a really good deal a few years ago,' she said.

'I monitor all statements and I even balance my cheque book,' Sally claims. 'But it's really difficult because Roger and I each have a cheque book.'

Sally and Roger don't visit the bank very often. For Sally — 'it's such a hassle; queues and parking. I get stressed sometimes but I do get on well with them.'

'I know that if I do a transaction which involves transferring money between accounts and taking out cash, that if I get it wrong I get charged an extra fee. I try to be careful but my husband hasn't a clue. He just deposits and withdraws whenever he feels like it. He usually gets it wrong. I can't tell you how many times he's overdrawn the account and had cheques bounce back on us.

'I don't know exactly how much I pay in fees, all I know is it's a very expensive and messy business. Otherwise we try to be as efficient as possible — paying into the credit card account each month and paying bills by phone whenever possible. I think my credit card has about $700 or $800 owing on it. And yes we bought that new gas heater a couple of months ago on the David Jones account and that's still outstanding. But I did pay $50 into the account last week.'

Sally concluded 'Yes, I am concerned about keeping this many accounts because of the number of fees and charges involved.'

Sound familiar? Sally is certainly efficient and careful. But she hasn't looked at simplifying her banking business. Nor has she analysed the real cost of running their banking. She and Roger know that bank fees and charges are part of life.

They would be shocked to learn that they are probably *losing* about $150 each month in *excess* fees and charges, and lost opportunity on interest rates, and that's *not* counting their Diners Club or American Express cards, each of which incur annual account fees and high interest rates. *That's $1800 a year down the drain; money that could go into the mortgage. Money to build wealth upon.* We'll examine how they should cut back these costs, but first look at the (monthly) fees they pay to the bank.

	Account-keeping fees	**Transaction fees**	**FID and BAD**	**Other***
cheque account (joint)	$5.00	$12.00	$14.78	$65.00
savings account (his)	$2.00	nil	$1.70	nil
savings account (hers)	$2.00	nil	$1.00	nil
savings account (theirs)	$2.00	nil	$1.80	nil
savings account (child 1)	$2.00	nil	$0.42	nil
savings account (child 2)	$2.00	nil	$0.42	nil
ATM ***	—	$3.00	—	—
bankcard (theirs)	$1.50	$9.00**	$2.85	nil

Note that the cheque account did *not* maintain a minimum balance of $500 during the month.

*This includes:

special clearance fee	$15.00
reference fee	$10.00
overdraw fees	$30.00
bounced inward cheque	$10.00

** interest on debit balances

*** includes three ATM withdrawals at another bank

Sally and Roger earned a total interest on all accounts of $287.00 for the year, made up as follows:

joint savings account; average balance $5000	$110.00
personal savings accounts (2); average balance $7000	$165.00
savings accounts; average balance $800 each	$12.00

The average interest rate earned was 2.1per cent. By comparison the average yield available at a non-bank cash management trust for the same period was 6.25 per cent. This would have yielded $750.00 (excluding kids as this was below the minimum required balance of $2000). The 'opportunity loss' was therefore $475 ($750 – $275), or $40 per month.

Sally and Roger are typical — although not necessarily average — *high volume* account holders:

- 6 ATM withdrawals from own machine
- 3 ATM withdrawals from other bank machines
- 8 Eftpos, 6 card purchases
- 10 cheque withdrawals
- 3 OTC withdrawals
- 1 periodic payment to home loan
- 4 direct debits
- 3 cheque deposits (on one slip)
- 3 cheque deposits requiring separate slips
- 4 direct credits.

How Sally and Roger could reduce the impact of fees and charges

- Close all unnecessary accounts. If Sally and Roger insist on the luxury of running 'private' individual accounts they should identify these as *low* activity accounts, leaving a minimum deposit of $500 in each at all times. These would incur little or no fees.
- Keep $500 in the account at all times and if they must have a cheque facility Sally and Roger should open up a transaction account — a *high volume* account — to minimise transfers and save on government taxes.
- Keep within fee-free threshold counting all Eftpos, ATM, cheques, and over-the-counter transactions.
- At all times use own bank ATMs.
- Plan their banking: use one cheque book only; keep withdrawals to a minimum. Sally and Roger can save money by withdrawing fewer large amounts than lots of smaller amounts.
- Avoid using cheques to pay bills: use Eftpos, credit card or phone, or direct debits.
- Withdraw cash only two or three times a month.
- Children's accounts can be fee-free if nominated as 'held on behalf of ...'

Sally and Roger, who last month paid fees to the bank of $105, should be able to slash this down to $12 to $15. The $23 paid in government taxes, should, with good planning, cut back to about $6 to $12.

The golden rule is: don't be complacent — inertia can be costly. Change bad habits. Sally and Roger may have had a bad month with accounts overdrawn and higher than normal penalties, but their case, while obviously excessive, is by no means extreme. Even a single person with a single account needs to *manage* his or her banking business to avoid unnecessary fees and charges.

What Sally and Roger's case demonstrates is how easily active family banking can run up heavy and crippling costs. Getting a handle on the fees and taxes you pay leads the way to reducing fees on a transaction or savings account. *Get intimate with your bank account, not your bank.*

By operating too many accounts or choosing the wrong account you are throwing away hundreds of dollars each year. This may not be a fortune, and although individual savings are not large they are likely to be a sizeable sum each year. Such savings will make achieving your financial goals much easier.

One of the questions arising from Sally and Roger's experience is the issue of interest on savings and transactions accounts. We will look more closely at this in Chapter 5 but for the moment let's look at the interest paid on transaction accounts to illustrate how banks slug you mercilessly.

Interest on the transaction account: don't bank on it

Interest paid on transaction accounts with cheque facilities is generally so miserly as to be insignificant. They are based on a sliding scale ranging from 0 per cent for small amounts to around 6 per cent for amounts over $100 000.

The way most people use them, standard transaction accounts lose more in fees and charges (including government taxes) than they earn in interest. Interest is not so much a source of savings growth as a partial offset to the charges imposed!

Obviously, the higher rates offered by the banks for the larger deposits are designed to attract more money to the account. Check the rate offered for the amount you keep in the account. And remember that interest is usually calculated on a daily basis, while fee exemptions are determined on a minimum monthly balance.

The money earned in interest could be credited to your account monthly, quarterly, six monthly or annually, depending on which bank you are with. Obviously, the more frequent the payment the better. Once interest is added to the account it can accrue interest itself. Although only marginal this *interest on interest* (or compounding) can give an effective interest rate higher than the nominal or quoted rate. Ask your bank how interest is calculated.

But does bank interest matter?

Not when you are dealing with amounts of a few hundred dollars. You're better off here maintaining a minimum balance on your transaction account and avoiding the fees. Remember that in terms of genuine long-term savings the interest rate must be above the annual inflation rate for the savings to maintain their real value. With most banks paying between 0 and 2.5 per cent for deposit accounts you need to re-think what you really need to do about your *savings*.

In most cases — for accounts with balances up to around $1000 — the interest earned would fail to keep up with inflation and account costs (including government charges). This means that your money is losing its *real* value over time. Savings should not be kept in a transactions account.

Remember that the interest you earn on your accounts is a form of income and therefore subject to income tax. But the good news is that some fees and charges are tax-deductable as they are *expenses* you incur in the earning of this income.

This is one good reason for keeping your account statements — to keep track of fees and charges for taxation purposes. The *Tax Pack* provided by the Australian Taxation Office usually has a section in it giving information on the tax deductibility of account fees. Again, these items may appear small on each individual statement, but they can contribute to a sizeable reduction in income tax due on interest earned. For example, if you pay tax of 43 per cent on every extra dollar of interest earned, deductable fees and charges of $250 will save you $107 in tax for the year.

The other good news concerning tax on interest is that you may be able to avoid it entirely if you structure your finances correctly. (See Chapter 8 for the details.) If you have long-term savings then you will need to look at getting the most for your money. Read Chapter 13 for a guide.

Tip offs to rip-offs

- Avoid one-off bank charges — such as special clearances — they can be very steep. And don't overdraw your account!
- Close all unnecessary accounts — combine your accounts — you may find it easier to maintain the minimum monthly balance if you combine several accounts with lower balances into one.
- Find out what your bank's fee-free threshold is and plan your banking habits around it.
- At all times only use your own bank's ATM.
- Bank interest paid on transactions accounts are generally miserly. If you have $2000 or more in the account, shop around for a better deal.

Chapter 4

First steps in taking on the banks

Dorothy has had the power to her home cut off after she forgot to pay the electricity bill. She regularly loses her cheque book. And even when she is supposed to be saving the temptation to have just one more dinner with friends is often too strong. And despite the fact that she is a successful executive at a firm of architects, she can never carry more than $50 cash in her wallet for fear of blowing it in an unplanned spending spree.

Getting control of your finances

It is somehow reassuring to hear Dorothy's story because it may sound familiar. While her finances are not out of control Dorothy is a long way from being in control of her money. She's not really all that different from Sally and Roger or most other people. There is no real financial plan — just dealing with the bills and commitments as they arise. This means nobody is making choices that are theirs to make about finances. And choice brings its own rewards.

Meanwhile real hard-earned cash is being eroded by bank fees and charges and poor banking practices. Thousands of dollars are frittered away each year. Converting this opportunity into reality won't happen without some action that demands a more organised approach to finances and banking.

In this chapter we'll look at where does the money go? How to make a money management plan and easy steps to budgeting. You'll be amazed at how much easier the battle against the banks becomes once you work to a plan. We all know the painful truth: unless you can control your finances there‘s no hope for financial independence and security — only financial purgatory.

Where does the money go?

The plaintive plea of today. Who's to blame for our personal financial woes? Blame the banks? Not this time.The economy? Again not this time. A weak economy means job insecurity and that limits spending. However, there has been a blowout in household debt. We're spending money on a whole raft of new products, such as mobile phones and computers, putting our pay packets under pressure.

According to Australian Bureau of Statistics figures close to 17 per cent of household income — that means for each and every one of us — goes to servicing debt in the form of credit card interest, mortgages and other loans. This figure has apparently risen dramatically over the past few years and shows no sign of abating.

This time there is no one to blame but ourselves. Part of the problem is that there are now so many credit cards available we have all become vulnerable to making purchases we can't afford. There are over 100 different cards on the market with Australians being among the biggest consumer of cards of any country in the world.

With card providers showering us with bonus points every time we buy something, we're all tempted to buy everytime we go into a store. More so since recent slumps in the retail industry have meant bargains galore in everything from clothing and electical goods to cars.

Even the home market, with real estate being flat and interests rates low, beckons. Temptation is everywhere; for example, cheaper holidays due to competition between the airlines and frequent flyer points. With all the luxuries of the world on display — new cars, swimming pools, electrical goods — those hot, little credit cards burn a hole in our pockets. Who can say no?

On a national level the figures have also reflected the increasing trend to gambling with each state now boasting casinos and more advertising dollars spent promoting TAB, Lotto, Pools and Keno. Lets face it. We, the poor consumers, have no chance! It seems that close to every second household in Australia is out there having a flutter while at the same time ruining the household budget.

We can all identify with these money-eating fads. Despite massive falls in interest rates over the past five years, we are under greater and greater pressure to make ends meet — and more often than not this means using credit to bridge the gap.

Managing our personal finances paves the way not only to reducing debt but also to building wealth.

Here is an example of a typical family's annual expense sheet as a first step towards a money management plan. (Later we will look at how Joe and Jenny could use some simple tricks to better manage their money.)

Joe and Jenny average: family income $60 000

Net income (salary, wages and interest)	$48 000
Expenditure	
Fixed (rent, mortgage, car repayments)	$19 200
Variable (food, clothing, fares)	$19 300
Discretionary (gifts, entertainment, holiday, sport)	$10 500
Total expenditure	$49 000
Funds available for savings or investment	$ nil

The bottom line: In their $49 000 yearly expenditure — $1000 more than they earn — Joe and Jenny spend several thousand dollars a year in interest on their car loan, personal loan repayments and credit card interest. Not that exceptional. But at this rate, they will not succeed in creating for themselves a financially independent future.

Speak to any self-made person and the story is the same: the key to financial security is to be (ultimately) debt free. And the secret of achieving this is through budgeting — knowing where your money goes, not every year, not every month, but every day. It may sound hard and boring, but it's simple and it will ultimately be rewarding. Getting organised is the first step.

How organised are you?

Are you organised? Are you ready to take on the responsibility of planning, budgeting and saving? Most of us don't get into the swing of things unless we have to. Let's look at Stephanie's story as a case in point:

Stephanie shopped at the local 7 Eleven. Not because it had the best range, nor the best prices — her husband always reminded her that they were at least 33 per cent more expensive than Franklins — but because she could drive up to the front door, dash inside, get cash out of the ATM and buy whatever she needed.

Stephanie was a 'freelance' pharmacist, working in a number of pharmacies around Brisbane's inner suburbs. She earned good money. Between her husband's income as a teacher and her's they earned enough to support a $120 000 mortgage and a reasonable lifestyle. So Stephanie never thought about budgets; savings were what was left over after the bills were paid.

Then the baby arrived. Looming large were the costs of day care and a new, larger home. And, of course, a very big hole in their finances with Stephanie off work for six months or so.

Money dried up rapidly and soon a whole new reality dawned upon them. They would need to plan, and spending needed to be watched.

The first thing to go was the 7 Eleven.

'I had to concede that we were spending thousands of dollars extra for the convenience,' she said.

Next was their banking. It was a chaotic mess of accounts and paper. 'We decided to rationalise our banking, knowing that there were hundreds of dollars blown away in bank interest and fees. Planning and discipline had to come into our lives.'

Quiz

1 Are you always running late in the mornings?
2 Are your cheque butts filled in?
3 Do you have unpaid parking fines?

If these questions ring a bell with you at all, you must wonder what causes your wheels to spin. But you are capable of setting your life in order. Ask yourself this: when you've paid the butcher, the baker, the grocer and the banker, who is left? Who is at the end of the queue? You!

Try putting yourself at the front of the queue, rather than at the end. Place your savings/investment at the *top*. This chapter will show you how.

The mechanics of money

'I make a fair income. I don't splash out on custom-made suits or fly first class, so why am I always this side of the poverty line?'

Despite my friend George's lament, extravagance, however, is generally not the problem. For families or households with high income, conspicuous spending on motor vehicles, household items and meals in restaurants is more likely to be an indication of a low ability to achieve financial security rather than a high ability. Conspicuous consumers don't get rich.

More to the point are the nagging day-to-day questions you can't answer: 'Why can other people at my income level afford more expensive vacations or larger homes? How can I use my money to provide a generally more satisfying life?'

Once you put your mind into gear and think ahead — all the time — about what you are going to have to spend each month, and you're budgeting effectively, the future will not be as fraught with financial disasters at every turn. It's the financial messes that burn money. Not lack of income.

The key is to complete your plan, no matter how many times it needs to be adjusted. Once you know what you have to earn, spend and achieve in the next few weeks, years and long-term future you have put the finishing touches to the road that leads where you ultimately want to go.

A successful, self-made client came to see me for advice with several hundred thousand dollars to invest in a share portfolio. He was not your typical retiree. He was a 40-year-old tradesman who was not only careful with his money, but had plans extending way beyond the next pay cheque.

'You should be doing something with your disposable income to ensure you are saving it to create assets and wealth.

'You need to get control of your finances; attempt to have your debt in one place, at one rate of interest, instead of all over the place.

'If you get near retirement and you haven't done the planning beforehand, you won't have the money to live on when you need it.'

That was John speaking, not me.

John had just sold a half share in his plumbing supplies business to two of his employees, and, looking ahead to retirement, decided that a share portfolio put in place now would guarantee him an income to support their retirement. He claimed that financial planning needs to start as early as possible in a working life.

'An ongoing disciplined approach is needed during working years.'

John sat opposite my desk. I suggested that the tables should be turned around. He had all the answers.

Some do's and don'ts of money management

- Start planning early, preferably when you first get a job. But don't despair, it's never too late!
- Keep your debt in one place, at one rate of interest.
- Pay off credit cards in time. Use credit cards for purchasing durable items such as cars, furniture or clothes. At least they last longer than your last restaurant meal.
- Use borrowings to purchase appreciables such as shares, a home or other investments.

- Set aside time at the beginning of each month to manage personal finances (one person to take charge).

However:

- Don't use credit cards as a source of loans — and never use them to pay interest on another loan. They've got very high interest rates.
- Don't have lots of smaller debts. Consolidate them. Keep the mortgage separate from the rest.
- Don't wait 'till schooling starts to plan for your children's school fees.

Your money management plan

As a first step in establishing your plan consider this: your plan revolves around the age and stage in life you're at. This may sound simple and too general for your specific needs, but here are some ideas and possible goals for each age group:

20 – 30	Establish credit: open a charge and credit card Open a bank account Set aside 10 per cent of income as savings
30 – 40	Purchase a primary residence Establish an education fund for the kids Establish a superannuation fund Budget and rearrange finances to keep control
40 – 50	Pay off primary residence Actively manage savings Pursue other interests: money isn't everything!

50 – 65 Plan for retirement
Enjoy life!

Budgets change as we go through different stages of our lives. Savings and spending patterns do vary. The *budget* we set needs to be flexible in this regard. So, instead of feeling we are failing our budgets it's OK to revise them to suit a new set of conditions — and to keep revising. This will give you a strong sense of control.

Being realistic with earnings and spending is the first step towards financial responsibility and control of your life. You must be accountable. You can't blame outside factors — not even the banks — if you aren't able to budget for your income and expenses.

Budgeting — yuk!

The very word conjures up images of hopelessness and despair. If you're like me you'll turn off at the very notion of counting your spending every day. We are, after all, a nation of borrowers rather then savers and we somehow feel miserly and impoverished if we need to count our pennies. But we're not talking about pennies we're talking about big bucks and control.

And yes, it's a sad fact, most people don't have a budget — and even if they do it's usually prepared once a year, looked at twice and then forgotten until the following year. But, the irony is, we all want one; we desperately want to feel like we're in control because, deep down, we all know that if we don't have one, we'll not only fritter away savings but waste money in unnecessary bank fees and charges.

Simple steps to a budget

Your budget should cover income (from all sources) and expenses for everything. In other words, you need to make a list of all the income you receive through salary, interest, pensions, government allowances and maintenance payments.

The next list to make is one that covers all the expenses you have. To simplify this — because it is not easy to anticipate all expenses — list expenses under three categories:

1 *Fixed* amounts such as mortgage and insurance payments and any other amounts that don't alter.
2 *Essential* items such as food and groceries, clothing, telephone and electricity, or anything else which you have some control over.
3 *Non-essential* items such as entertainment, alcohol and cigarettes, newsagency purchases, holidays, baby-sitting costs etc.

A simple budget sheet

An easy-to-complete month-by-month annual budget sheet is presented here as a starting point (see pages 278–9). You won't even have to think about where the money goes — simply following the headings. They will give you a clear indication of spending patterns and show you where surplus income could be used.

If you don't have a handle on all the items, don't worry. If you follow the steps outlined in the next section it will only take you a few weeks of receipt and docket-gathering to be in control.

A little preparation is necessary to get started

It's much easier to keep all your money-related information in the one place. All receipts for payments should be kept in a file.

The best place to start laying the groundwork for your budget is to determine who will be the record keeper. If you are single this is not an issue. In a relationship one person is usually better than two — if you want to protect the relationship and the budget! This person will deposit cheques, pay the bills and balance the cheque book.

Next set the framework for the budget around your principle source of income — usually a wage or salary (or two) and, if monthly, a monthly based budget will work best. If fortnightly, a two-weekly based budget should be used, and so on.

Budgeting: the monthly routine

This routine applies to everyone: on or near the first of the month balance the chequebook and pay the bills taking care that the minimum balance does not fall below the minimum amount needed to qualify for a fee-free account at the bank.

The paper work

1 Collecting

(a) Bills, bank statements, bank deposit slips and anything to do with money that enters during the month. Put them in the folder and make sure you save all sales slips for purchases and keep them in the money folder.
(b) Payment booklets for car or mortgage repayments — keep them in the money folder.
(c) Cheque book for payments — keep permanently near or in folder.

2 Sorting out

Divide the contents into five piles:

(a) Banking statements, cancelled cheques, deposit slips and any other bank notices.
(b) Bills, renewal notices and any correspondence which will require payment by cheque or phone.
(c) Payment booklets for regular debts.
(d) All sales slips and cash register slips.
(e) Anything else such as term deposit notices.

3 Reconcile the bank statements

Even the sound of this is frightening, but it is a fact of life that banks do make mistakes (see Chapter 1).

I know of someone who was accidentally credited with $900 instead of $90. The mistake was not picked up by either party for a while. Unfortunately, the person drew a number of cheques against this credit, only to find they bounced when the bank corrected the mistake.

The outcome cost the customer over $100 in dishonour fees. To make matters worse, one of the payments was to a credit card company who referred the matter to the Credit Reference Bureau, therefore affecting the person's credit rating. It took a lot of effort to correct this mess.

- Put the most recent bank statement in front of you and start from the top cheque butt and tick off the amount from the statement. Continue until finishing the cheque butts. Now reconcile these by listing non-presented cheque amounts under the debit amount.
- Add the account-keeping fees if applicable (for example, some banks now charge a $5 a month account fee) and add government charges (BAD and FID) — use the figure from an earlier statement. Add any other charges, for example, special charges such as a new cheque book or fee for handling a bounced cheque.
- Make sure no other amounts remain unticked. This could be someone else's cheque added to your account.
- Select the deposit slips that register on this month's statement and mark them off in your cheque book as you did with the cheques. Add the deposit slips that did not appear on this month's statement, plus your balance on the closing date of the statement. Subtract the total amount of cheques outstanding from the sum you arrived at in the preceding step.

- The remainder should confirm your cheque book balance. If there is a small discrepancy, say up to $10, you may generally assume that the bank's computers are accurate and that you have made an error on your cheque stubs.
- At this stage, it would be a good idea to put this collection of paper back in the statement envelope and mark the month on the front. You may wish to separate items that are relevant to your tax return and put these in a tax file.
- Turning to the payment of bills: check the sales slips for department store and credit card purchases against their statements. Write a cheque for each bill, except for those accounts that can be paid by telephone with a credit card. Always fill in your cheque butt in full.
- By collecting all bill stubs and checkout receipts etc. and filing these away each month you have a good idea of how you are going on budget.
- For fixed obligations: take out your payment booklets. Write cheques for all items listed (loans, instalment payments, savings deposits etc.) and wait. If it is a payment month send the cheque.

The paperwork is not complicated. It takes the following steps:

- Select a monthly date for handling all financial obligations.
- Assemble everything you need.
- Sort all paper work into 5 piles.
- Reconcile your bank statements with your chequebooks.
- Write cheques for the bills.
- Collect all bill stubs and sales slips in an envelope and file away.
- Write cheques for fixed obligations.

Many people are intimidated by the mechanics of money. They feel the same intimidation whenever they need to deal with a bank.

One of my clients — a wealthy young woman — never knew the amount of her bank balance. She was always mislaying her bills and lived with the threat of having services withdrawn or cut off at any moment. This lack of control affected her investment decisions. I eventually encouraged her to go elsewhere as her accounts were always in arrears. It was not possible to do business with her, despite her wealth.

She was not impoverished. She was merely out of control. A few hours per month would have been sufficient to take care of all her money transactions.

A sure-fire way of making your budget work

Use the technology that successful people and businesses employ: *a cash flow plan.*

Joe's and Jenny's cash flow plan

	Jan.	Feb.	Mar.	Apr.	May*	Jun.**
Total bills	3900	3800	3900	3800	4900	5200
Total income	4000	4000	4000	4000	4000	4000
Net surplus/(deficit)	100	200	100	200	(900)	(1200)
Opening balance	nil	100	300	400	600	(300)
Closing balance (Net cash left)	100	300	400	600	(300)	(1500)

*includes health insurance

**includes third-party insurance, registration and car insurance

Note the usefulness of that pile of receipts and sales slips. Now you will be able to realistically put figures in place. The critical item is the *net cash left* line. Watch for continuing negative results. Joe and Jenny's bank balance goes deeper and deeper into the red, by June sinking to $1500. This indicates a mismatch between income and spending patterns. Adjustments in spending may need to be made.

In the months where none of the big items fall due — for example, third-party insurance and car registration, or health insurance — a healthy cash figure should appear. Match this against your cash at bank (or in the pocket) at the beginning of the month to see how well (read accurately) you are going. If you are dreadfully far away, say hundreds of dollars, go back and do an analysis of any unusually high spends during the month. And watch those deficit months!

The cash flow plan works brilliantly over a full cycle; that is, where all your bills have fallen due, including the big or annual ones. You can see why it makes sense to pay bills such as water and council rates on a quarterly basis, thus spreading the load. Some insurance companies now allow for motor vehicle and other forms of insurance to be paid monthly.

Use this technique to your advantage: it will highlight unnecessary spending — such as large bank charges!

Tips to make bugeting easier

- Invest *extra* pay cheques. If you budget on four-weekly pay cheques per month, every thirteenth pay check is an extra. If you are paid fortnightly, there's an extra cheque each quarter. Include it in your budget as *savings* or *investment.*
- Limit impulse buying — leaving your credit card and cheque book at home.
- If you do make a credit card charge — register it in your cheque book as if you are making a purchase with a cheque and deduct the amount from your bank balance. Think of it — no more statement shock! No more plastic fantasy.

- Pay bills when due — to make the most of your money write the cheque for the bill as soon as it arrives, but don't mail it until its due.
- Treat windfalls such as bonuses or tax refunds as money for special purposes rather than impulse spending.
- Make savings a regular *expense* (this could go as an extra payment to the mortgage). Put yourself at the top of the queue!
- Allow for expenditures each period that require no accounting, for example, fun money or personal allowance.
- Don't try to keep track of every cent.
- Make one withdrawal from the ATM for the entire month to cover your general weekly cash expenses (keep those bank fees down).

Emergency money

One thing is certain. Life does not happen as you plan it. Just when you think you have accounted for everything and the bills are all paid, life kicks in and messes up your budget. The dog gets sick, the car breaks down, you have a lengthy illness, or some other natural disaster strikes. Your kids show musical talent and you need to invest big bucks in a saxophone or guitar or, the inevitable, they grow into teenagers and want their own car.

There are a couple of things you can do to avoid being caught by Murphy's Law: load the expenses side a little each month, thus siphoning off a little more to that *savings* account; or have a little item in the budget called *miscellaneous* and nominate an amount each month over and above the savings plan.

This amount is not for that new car or overseas holiday. It is a disaster fund and if you are lucky enough to have avoided a disaster for a few months you will probably have enough for the car repair bill or other expense that can hit you when you least expect it.

In Chapter 5 we will look at getting a real grip on your banking — not only for control but also to open up opportunities for profit.

Summary: five steps to taking control of your finances

- Make a money management plan: get started with a budget and adjust your budget continuously.
- Put yourself at the head of the queue: pay yourself and put the amount into a savings account.
- Set aside an hour each month to do the paper work. And please, one person per family as the keeper of the books!
- Use a cash flow plan to really get a handle on your finances.
- No more surprises: put aside under miscellaneous up to a couple of hundred dollars a month for any unplanned expenditure.

Chapter 5

Choosing the right account

Whether you are single, upwardly mobile, a single parent or married with children, what features do you need in a bank account? — credit card access, unlimited transactions, phone facilities or convenient locations? Or do you want the basic, fee-free transaction account? These are the questions we will be looking at to help you select the right account. But first a very real question.

To bank or not to bank? The non-bank alternative

Before looking at your banking needs we should ask: do you really want to deal with a bank or are you better suited to a non-bank?

Here are the alternatives:

- insurance companies
- credit unions

- building societies
- mortgage originators like Aussie Home Loans and RAMS
- cash management trusts

What are their roles?

- *Insurance companies.* Companies like Priority-One (an AMP subsidiary) and FAI will lend money for mortgages as well as personal loans.
  Advantage: Competitive rates and packages are offered.
  Disadvantage: While resembling banks more and more, they are generally not as accessible and not all will offer transaction-style account facilities.
- *Credit unions.* Will lend money — some for mortgages, all for cars and other personal loans. They offer the same transaction-style accounts as banks do.
  Advantage: They are very competitive and tend to have lower fee structures. Credit unions are owned by their members and are a viable alternative to the banks.
  Disadvantage: Credit Unions are not as secure as banks, nor as accessible; they have very few branches.
- *Building societies.* They are still reeling from the collapse of the Pyramid Group and from the conversion of many of the larger building societies like St George into banks. They are specialists in lending money for home loans and also offer the same transaction-style accounts as banks.
  Advantage: Competitive rates. MLC Building Society, for example, offers innovative home loan packages, and *all-in-one* accounts.
  Disadvantage: They are not as secure as banks and don't have as many branches.
- *Mortgage originators.* They will lend money for mortgages only. Loans are protected by insurance, so while the banks are traditionally safer, borrowers need not fear.
  Advantage: Very competitive rates are on offer.

Disadvantage: Like insurance companies you can't do all your banking through them.

- *Cash management trusts (CMT).* Trusts like Macquarie will manage your money for you. See Chapter 14 about this alternative way of having money looked after while in high-yielding accounts and still having the advantage of cheque books and transaction-style account facilities.

If you still believe the bank is your best alternative this chapter will help you find the account that's right for you. But first:

How intimate are you with your banking?

- What is your minimum monthly balance?
- How many transactions do you make a month?
- What's the mix of your transactions — ATMs, cheques or over-the-counter?
- How often do you go to your bank? Are your visits necessary?

If you could only answer one of these, congratulations. Most people wouldn't have a clue.

These questions are important for those seeking to control their finances. Not knowing the answers to any of these will certainly cost you money. And because no two banks' fee structures are the same, some homework is necessary if you really want to reduce the cost of your banking. *It is possible to achieve fee-free banking* but you have to *know* your account inside out. Remember, fees are on the up and up and by not changing your banking patterns you will pay the price.

You've seen how fees and charges can add up. Later in the chapter we will look at the key features you should consider in any account: the level of fees and charges, interest, accessibility and *extras*. Deciding on a transaction account requires not only a knowledge of the features offered but also your own banking behaviour.

The wrong account or bank can cost you hundreds of dollars a year in unnecessary charges.

Personal profiles

Jim — young and single (low balance, medium use)

Jim is 20 and just starting his working life. He has put aside some money so the temptation to raid it on spending splurges is reduced. Jim's balance is low for most of the year, and with a busy lifestyle and little banking experience, he occasionally goes into the red when writing cheques.

Minimum balance each month	$nil
Withdrawals per month	
ATMs, own bank	5
ATMs, other bank	3
Eftpos	3
Cheques written	4
Over-the-counter withdrawals (card)	2
Deposits per month:	
Direct credits (pay)	1
Cheques received	0
One-offs per year	
Bank cheques	1
Bounced outward cheques*	1

*Note that most banks charge either dishonour fees (up to $35 per cheque) or an interest charge of up to 18.75 per cent for 'accidental overdraw'. Accidental overdraw charges are generally much lower with credit unions — usually about $5.

Peter and Paula — family (medium balance, high use)

Peter and Paula have quite a lot of money flowing into and out of their account, as it receives two incomes and copes with the expenses of running a household of four people.

Minimum balance each month (by design)	$500
Withdrawals per month	
ATMs, own bank	4
ATMs, other bank	2
Eftpos	3
Cheques written	7
Over-the-counter withdrawals (card)	3
Deposits per month	
Direct credits (pay)	2
Cheques received	2
One-offs per year	
Bank cheques	2
Bounced inward cheques	1

Jenny — single, professional, well-off (high balance, medium use)

Jenny is a high income earner. Although she has a range of investments elsewhere, she likes to keep a healthy balance in her transaction account as it gives her flexibility. Unlike Jim or Peter and Paula, Jenny does not have to worry about bouncing a cheque!

Minimum balance per month	$5000
Withdrawals per month	
ATMs, own bank	4
ATMs, other bank	2
Eftpos	6
Cheques written	6
Over-the-counter withdrawals (card)	2

Deposits per month	
Direct credits (pay)	1
Cheques received	3
One-offs per year	
Bank cheques	1

The bad news for Jim is there no *good* bank transactions account for someone with a low balance and who makes a lot of transactions each month. But there could be good news if he limits the number of transactions — some banks won't impose a transaction charge if you are under 21. Otherwise, he would incur charges of between $5 to $12 a month (plus dishonour fees) — probably costing him well over $100 a year.

Jim could consider moving to a credit union, but he would ultimately be better off saving $500 and running a fee-free account at the bank. It would not only save him fees but he would avoid dishonoured cheque costs because he'd need to be a little more disciplined towards his banking habits.

The most important consideration for active account users such as Peter and Paula is to avoid transaction fees based on the high volumes. The good news is that Peter and Paula can avoid fees and charges with a minimum balance of $500 at all times. Based on their usage, they need a transaction account which will offer them at least 24 free transactions a month (for example, 20 electronic and four over-the-counter or cheque withdrawals). Here a $5 monthly account-keeping fee usually applies.

A number of banks will not impose fees on transactions. Most banks will offer an account which requires a minimum balance. You will need to ask for a *transaction free* account.

Peter and Paula need to take care because failure to keep above this minimum balance could cost them over $200 a year in bank fees alone. They also need to take care because excess withdrawal fees of over $1 and 65 cents for electronic transactions will also apply.

As far as Jenny is concerned a high balance makes all the difference. She is avoiding most fees but her healthy balance means that she is *losing* out on hundreds of dollars each year in interest. She should select an account which offers a combination of low fees and high interest rates. Interest rates offered on transaction accounts are generally low, usually around 1 per cent for amounts of between $500 and $5000. Most banks, however, now offer *bonus* interest points of up to 3 per cent under certain conditions. But you need to ask for it. We will look at where accounts like Jenny's could make better returns on their money below.

Of these three profiles select the one which best describes your banking habits. If you fall outside these stereotypes — for example, if you are a single parent — choose a profile which best describes your own. The next step is to:

Determine your needs

Like money, transaction accounts are one of the necessities of financial life. We need an account to which our salary can be electronically transferred, since most employers insist on this arrangement, as does, for example, the Department of Social Security when paying pensions or benefits.

All customers want *convenience* — some are even prepared to forgo many other features just to be able to slip quickly into their local bank branch.

When Marie decided to open a term deposit at a new bank, she noted there was a customer car park at the rear of the building. 'This was an important consideration; I have young children, and lack of parking makes for a whole new deal in terms of time.'

How convenient or accessible is your bank? Is there a branch nearby? Are the ATMs convenient? A survey conducted by one of the banks late last year found that only one in three people prefer to do most or all of their bank business inside a branch. Perhaps it's the queues?

Although location is often a consideration when choosing a bank — you don't want to spend an hour making a deposit — it should not be your primary reason for going with one bank over another. Good service and reasonable rates should be.

Are low fees important to you? If they are, with minimum fees being at least $5 to $20 monthly for a personal account, you can't afford not to research fees and minimum balances. Comparison shopping is the key. Choose at least two banks and one credit union and compare their fees and services — for *your* particular style of banking.

Extras such as telephone bill-paying may be an added convenience factor, and may become a mandatory feature as bank queues get longer. Other features such as restaurant discounts or travel insurance discounts may be irrelevant to your needs.

Account features

- statement record of transactions
- at-call funds (no restrictions on access to your money)
- a limited number of free cheques
- a plastic card (for ATM and Eftpos)
- bill-paying facilities
- frequent interest payments
- interest calculated on daily balance
- credit card access
- a phone banking option
- minimum balance for fee free usage

Keep in mind when assessing any extras that the basic cost of the account is likely to have a bigger impact than any extras you get — don't be sucked in by cute ad-ons without considering the fees and charges. Remember that someone has to pay for the 'frills', not to mention the expensive advertisements — and it won't be the bank!

Which account will it be?

With 50 banks and over 300 building societies and credit unions around Australia offering up to a dozen or more variations in transaction and savings accounts, the choices are never-ending. You can certainly be forgiven for doing nothing! But there are easy solutions.

Simple banking is available at a number of banks without the penalty of high account fees or high transaction charges. But take care, because some banks will always charge for big users of cheques. Citibank, for example, charges a monthly fee of $5 *and* a $2 fee for every withdrawal in excess of 20 a month.

No-frills fee-free banking with the Big Four

Fee-free banking is no longer just for the wealthy. It is available to most people. But it takes some planning and a lot of discipline. And although the savings are not huge, they are significant and offer you a more disciplined and planned approach to your banking.

Remember there *are* alternatives to bank accounts: credit unions, for example.

Taking the initiative — or the battle to the banks — is superb training for making a real difference where it counts. Managing your money and working the system to your advantage is what this game is all about.

But, before ditching your bank heed the action plan, which should take care of your personal wish list.

Bank	Account	Number of free transactions each month	Excess usage charges
ANZ	Acess simplicity	6 (including max. 2 OTC*)	$1.25 for each OTC transaction 40c for ATM, Eftpos
Commonwealth Bank	Basic	6 (including 4 OTC)	$1.50 for OTC 45c for ATM, Eftpos
National Australia Bank	FlexiAccount	8 (including 4 cheque or OTC)	$1.00 for OTC and cheque 25c for ATM, Eftpos, telephone banking
Westpac**	Basic	6 withdrawals	$1.00 for OTC 65c for ATM, Eftpos

*OTC: over-the-counter

**No cheque book, statements 6-monthly

Action Plan

Find out what fees and charges apply to your account. Ask your branch for a full list if you're not sure — it should be readily available.

Check the bank fees on your statement to see how much they cost each month.

2DEC96	
MONTHLY TRANSACTION SUMMARY	
DEPOSITS/ITEMS LODGED	4
CHEQUE/COUNTER WITHDRAWALS	6
NATIONAL ATM/EFTPOS WDLS/VISACASH TFRS	3
NON-NATIONAL ATM WITHDRAWALS/ENQUIRES	0
OTHER WITHDRAWALS	0
VISACASH RELOAD TRANSFERS	0
TRANSACTION FEE	$2.00
TOTAL ACCOUNT FEES	$2.00

ACCOUNT FEES		2.00
CREDIT TAX	$6.70	
DEBITS TAX	$7.80	
		14.50

Work out what fees affect you the most. Be prepared to take action, be it closing accounts, opening new ones or moving to another non-bank financial institutions such as a building society or a credit union if the fees that are hitting you hardest aren't charged.

And, please, one cheque book per account only!

Close all unnecessary accounts. Consolidate them into a single account. Try and maintain your balance at above the minimum level (usually $500). Most families can make do with only one transaction account. It should be evident from some of the horror stories we've seen that keeping small amounts in numerous accounts is not productive.

Special purpose accounts — such as children's savings, education funds, a *buffer* or overseas trip — if absolutely necessary, need to have minimum balances to avoid fees. If the balance is above, say, $2000, the money should be put away on term deposits or cash management trusts. Some banks will not charge account-keeping fees on accounts held in trust for a child. So, open up this type of account for your child's savings.

Check transaction fees. How many free transactions can you make each month? Note that transactions cover almost every banking activity, for example, ATMs and Eftpos, phone banking, not only the writing of cheques.

- ATM use is often cheaper than over-the-counter transactions, although check this if your account is with a credit union.
- Use the ATMs belonging to your own bank — most charge for the use of other ATMs, usually from 20 cents up to $1 a time.

Tip: Using Eftpos to pay for purchases can help you avoid an extra withdrawal from your bank or ATM if you draw out extra cash. Most banks charge between 25 and 60 cents for each Eftpos use.

Use *direct debits* to pay your bills. Most life and health insurance companies and others will make automatic deductions (that is, direct debits) from your transaction account if arrangements are made. By paying bills by direct debit, you'll ensure that your regular bills are paid on time. You can forget about payment dates. And remember direct debit withdrawals are free.

Fee exemptions. You may be exempt from some fees if you have a loan (home, personal or a credit card) as long as the loan is at the same bank as your account. A wide range of fee exemptions apply to many accounts. The exemptions vary as to which fees you won't have to pay.

To see if you qualify for any exemptions, ask your bank for a list — they rarely go out of their way to alert you to all of them. For example, people under the age of 18 or tertiary students or pensioners usually attract exemptions from most of the large banks.

Negotiate. If you don't ask, you'll never know whether a bank is willing to negotiate on any of its fees. Make sure you inquire — some of the most popular concessions the banks are prepared to make are fee waivers, free cheques or ATM cards. For example, some banks will waive their fee if you attach a Visa debit card to the account. But you need to ask.

Good housekeeping. We've looked at the value of good housekeeping as far as money is concerned in Chapter 4.

- Keep track of your account balance — fill in that cheque butt! — as accidentally overdrawing can be very expensive, especially when writing cheques. Take care of direct debits: fill in the cheque butt at the beginning of each month for direct debits such as periodical payments.

- Don't throw out statements of the past year; you may need them later for tax or accounting purposes, and you may be charged for replacements.

Some fee-free schemes allow, for example, up to 30 cheques free of charge. But don't let this happen to you: Mary was charged a small fee for the 32nd cheque. At 33 cheques she realised that she had been charged for all 33!

Take care to keep within the specified limit on number of cheques and, of course, minimum balances.

The humble savings account: do we need one?

Clearly the most important feature of savings accounts tends to be the interest rate, as accessibility on a short-term basis is generally not an issue. Age and stage is important. For example, if you are aged between, say, 25 and 39, and saving for a home, then savings is probably the most important feature of your life.

In an attempt to win over customers being lost to the banks through higher rates being available elsewhere, banks are also adding sweeteners. Savings accounts have come a long way. Look, for example, at the sample on the next page, taken from a flier for Westpac's Bonus Saver account.

Features	**Benefits**
Competitive interest rates	Westpac Bonus Saver pays you an extra 3% p.a. interest on all your savings when you make at least one deposit and no withdrawals in a calendar month.
Bank safety	Not only does Westpac Bonus Saver offer competitive interest rates but deposits are invested with Australia's oldest bank.
Interest calculation and payment	Interest is calculated daily on the full balance and paid to the account six-monthly, every March and September.
Access to your money	With Westpac Bonus Saver you have instant access to your money without notice, even through Automatic Teller Machines at any time, day or night (personal customers only). You also have the convenience of banking over the phone through Westpac Telephone Banking.
Making the most of your Bonus Saver	You have the flexibility of being able to have regular savings paid directly into your Bonus Saver Account. You can arrange for a fixed amount to be deposited into your Bonus Saver on a regular basis: weekly, fortnightly or monthly. This can be direct from your salary, from another Westpac account or from an account you have with another financial institution.

Most of the banks today have promoted the idea of *bonus* savings accounts, where extra interest points are offered for customers who make regular deposits and few withdrawals.

With the bonuses customers can now earn interest up to 6 per cent on their savings, which is much higher than rates available on normal transaction accounts (see the following comparative table for a $5000 deposit).

	Return p.a. (%)
Bank savings accounts 'at call'	
NAB National Passbook	1.00
Westpac Passbook Saver	1.25
Term deposits	
ANZ 30 day	3.85
Westpac	4.85
*Cash management trusts**	
Macquarie	5.92
Perpetual	5.97

* *Rates are annual percentage returns based on returns over the latest 7-day period*

Customers whose accounts continue to earn bonus interest for six consecutive months become eligible for a range of discounts, with some banks making offers that include 0.25 per cent off the standard personal loan rate, and no establishment fee on a home loan.

Savings for short to medium term purposes — the holiday, the renovation, the new car or emergency funds — can certainly go into term deposits, special savings accounts, cash management trusts or credit unions. However, when it comes to long-term returns there are other issues to take into account.

Consider, for example, what happens if you put $10 000 into a term deposit. You could earn a return of up to $600 over 12 months. However, at the end of the twelve months you would lose up to 43 per cent (assuming you earn $40 000 a year): $258 to tax and 3 per cent or $300 to inflation. This deposit would leave you with a real return of $42 — or a rate of 0.4 per cent. Also, many who earn more than $1000 interest on their bank accounts may be subject to provisional tax, which can further erode real returns.

Strategies that preserve the real value of your savings and ones that can grow them in real terms are the subject of Chapter 14. Generally these strategies do not involve leaving your money in the bank!

Alternatives to the savings account

Falling interest rates have encouraged investors to turn to cash management trusts where rates have traditionally been much higher than bank deposit rates. They allow withdrawals within 24 hours, and have proved themselves to be secure.

The managers of cash management trusts are often banks or large insurance companies. The disadvantage of cash management trusts is that their rates tend to move more or less in tandem with prevailing short-term interest rates, whereas term deposits are fixed at a rate for the *term*.

One solution for most would be to keep a transaction account for everyday expenses in addition to the cash management trust account.

High tech savings account

Why earn interest only on your savings — on what's left over? Why not put your whole salary to work earning money market rates of interest from the day it hits your account? And why not achieve this without bank fees eroding the balance?

A number of cash management trusts now offer the ability to run household expenses out of the account simply by arranging all regular budgeted expenses such as loan repayments and insurance to be paid automatically.

Add regular savings to the account as a buffer and other payments such as health care, holidays, renovations and home improvement can be funded as the expense arises and cheques drawn. Grocery or petrol expenses, for example, can be charged to the credit card account and settled by direct debit, monthly. Cash is available on ATM.

Look at the benefits:
Assume: savings of $8000.
The household earns an average of $5000 per month.
All budgeted monthly expenses total $3000.

If $8000 is invested in a savings account that earns 2.75 per cent, the interest on this amount would be $220 for the year.

By investing $8000 in the CMT, interest on the accumulating balance each month brings in $846.40, based on an average interest yield of 5.7 per cent.

Significant amounts can be earned on amounts which may otherwise be deposited in a low interest/high transaction cost bank account.

This method of saving and budgeting can combine two types of accounts for many investors: a rainy day and a bank savings account.

Cheque accounts: who needs one?

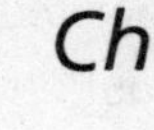

John was holidaying on the Gold Coast. Knowing he'd need spending money his employer deposited a cheque into John's ATM/savings account before he departed.

When he got to the Gold Coast, both the ATM and the bank teller refused John access to his money.

One of the most apparent and annoying failings of the banking system is the unconscionable delay in clearing cheques. Most banks quote a clearance time of *five working days*, but, let's be honest, this in reality means a week. A week to get access to your own money! People would definitely be justified in believing the bank's are rorting us. By holding on to their customers' money for longer than is necessary they are getting a cheap source of funding. (Although interest is credited from the day of deposit, most transactions accounts pay less than 1 per cent interest.)

Yet, every day about three million cheques worth more than $17 billion are written by individuals and businesses. Australians write 55 cheques per head every year, about a quarter the number written by Americans (237) — the greatest 'check' writers on earth. And despite predictions of the *cashless society*, and the advent of new banking technology, the cheque has survived as a convenient method of moving money around.

However, the use of cheques is declining as credit card transactions, Eftpos, direct credits and direct debits, and now telephone — or home — banking move into vogue. It's taken about 15 years, but cheques now account for a much reduced 38 per cent of non-cash payments. Although, we still write more cheques than we did 15 years ago.

The major reason given for holding a cheque account is it's convenience to pay bills. There is also the issue of security: cheques are *crossed* and have to be paid into a bank account and can't be cashed over the counter of a bank. To be absolutely secure you may also cross out the words 'or bearer' which appear on the cheque. This means the cheque has to be deposited into the account of the person to whom it has been made out.

The 'perfect' cheque account

'When you have a cheque account with Sydney Credit Union you won't have to pay activity fees, transfer fees, minimum monthly balance fees, maintenance fees, etc.

There are absolutely no credit union charges (most credit unions offer this). Only government charges and national bank fees (such as stop payment and cheque dishonour) apply. And if you are a pensioner your account is free from FID and BAD taxes as well.'

Of course, if you run any sort of business a cheque book is indispensable, while at the same time a record of the expenditure is available. And not only does it give you the ability to pay creditors and purchase goods, it is an easy way to arrange a line of credit or overdraft facility.

Cheques are no longer the all-purpose payment device they once were. But cheques remain popular because people are comfortable with them and because they remain the most convenient way to make certain kinds of payments: whether unplanned or spontaneous and for any amount at any time or place. But beware, the banks are likely to make us pay more for the convenience of cheques. Convenience always comes at a price.

The fact that most banks today offer *linked* accounts — that is, accounts which link the savings account with the transaction account and have ATM access as well — removes the necessity of having a separate cheque account. But do you need cheques at all?

Try cheque-free banking

Yes, pick yourself up from the floor. There can be life after a cheque book. Here's how it's done:

- Pay bills by credit card and settle the credit card account by transfers from your regular account.
- Arrange for direct debits from your accounts to pay regular bills, like your home loan.

- Use Eftpos at supermarkets and other retail outlets to pay directly from your account.
- Use ATMs for cash withdrawals.

What about that bill or two that can't be paid this way? When researching this book many people told me, 'I know it costs me but what about the *convenience*?'

The answer is simple. By all means bank *conveniently*, but know the alternatives which can be used without causing inconvenience. No one is suggesting walking around with a bundle of cash to pay the accounts. Just use the cheque book sparingly!

With the ever-increasing expansion of electronic banking, going without a cheque facility, although difficult for many today, may become normal practice in the future.

No more government taxes!

No cheque account means no BAD tax. Australians pay $1.8 billion a year — that's $100 for each person — in government financial transactions taxes. These are generally harder to avoid than bank fees, although having an account in Queensland will ensure you avoid FID, while having one in Canberra will allow you to escape BAD.

Lee, our young professional woman from Chapter 1, who *walked* to pay her bills may be adopting radical methods to avoid BAD (and bank charges), but she *does* save many dollars a year by taking her stand.

And note it's more than a question of not using cheques — you must have an account with *no* cheque facility at all. Even if you don't use a cheque book, if the account provides one you still face BAD charges on all withdrawals, including cash withdrawals from ATMs.

Janine banks with the ANZ. Her Access account allows her 15 free withdrawals per month. She operates a Visa card, linked to her transaction account for the purposes of transfers. She also operates a telephone banking facility with the bank, allowing her an additional avenue for paying bills, as well as statement information. Janine has no chequing facility.

She calculated last year that she paid more in state tax than she paid in bank charges! She now pays only $2–$4 in fees and taxes each month to operate her account.

'It's true that I have to carry around a little more cash to pay for things I would otherwise write a cheque for — I usually draw out $300 at a time. But I find that in the main, I can pay bills over the phone — either on credit card (credit card fees cost Janine approximately $15 a year) or by telephone banking.

'I can't begin to tell you how much time I save. I now spend less time at the bank and posting cheques. The hardest thing is resisting all those sales having all that cash in my wallet!'

Don't bank on bank cheques

My son Anthony sold his car last week, obtaining a bank cheque from the purchaser which he paid into his bank via an ATM. On the following Monday he went into his own branch of the NAB and asked if he could draw against it, and was told it would take five working days to clear. If he paid $15 he could get special clearance in 2 working days.

A few months ago Mrs J was asked to transfer $2500 direct to the bank account of a tradesman who was fitting new guttering to her suburban Sydney home. So she obtained a bank cheque and took it to a bank on the other side of the street. There she was told it would take some days to clear the cheque before their customer could utilise the funds.

Naturally Mrs J suggested that her cheque could be cleared at her bank branch if somebody cared to amble across the street with it. Her remark caused a great deal of fuss, with consultations between supervisors and other staff.

Finally, Mrs J had to go back to her own bank, have the cheque cancelled, and carry $2500 in cash across the street, a risky practice these days, and just what Mrs J tried to avoid in the first instance.

What is wrong with the system?

Apart from being extremely annoying, and all too common, these stories underline a myth which can get a lot of people into financial hot water: the belief that bank cheques are as good as cash. The fact is they aren't. While bank cheques are accepted for the most crucial transaction in most people's lives — the sale and purchase of the family home — this is more a matter of convention than a reflection of the bank cheque's unquestionable safety.

At the very least a bank cheque may be stopped where it has been forged or materially altered, lost or stolen. 'There are plenty of situations where a bank cheque can be dishonoured, so accepting it as payment is not without some risk,' cautions banker Bruce Terry, head of retail services for Macquarie Investment Management Limited.

And why, you may well ask, is a banker making this admission? Because 'There are some things that consumers should know,' Bruce Terry says. 'While the risk of being given a dud bank cheque in a property deal is very small, there is a bigger risk out there. It is the possibility of home buyers being caught short because a bank cheque they have deposited to their account, precisely in order to group funds for a property settlement, isn't cleared for a withdrawal in time for settlement day.'

And, as Terry points out, merely applying for speedier clearance doesn't guarantee it will be available in time. Although an issuing bank needs to authorise a speedier settlement, there is no guarantee that this will take place. It thus acts as a warning against relying on this particular facility even in the case of bank cheques.

What is interesting is that a bank always has the option to honour a bank cheque immediately it is deposited. Whether or not this happens will depend mainly on the relationship it has with each individual customer.

'Some banks allow instantaneous drawings against bank cheques,' Terry added. He notes, however, that banks usually seek confirmation from the issuing bank to establish that the details of the cheque are correct and that it has been properly issued, just as they do with personal cheques.

This is because under a number of circumstances a bank cheque can *bounce*; that is, be dishonoured. For example, a customer who ordered a bank cheque may have it stopped, perhaps because goods purchased turned out faulty or unsatisfactory.

Then there are those situations where a bank puts a stop on one of its bank cheques. This would occur where the customer concerned has paid for it with a personal cheque which has been drawn against uncleared or insufficient funds, presuming, of course, that they hadn't checked before issuing.

And, of course, there is fraud. For example, where a bank cheque is fraudulently altered, say by changing the amount from $1000 to $10 000. Or where the cheque itself is forged. A stop payment or dishonour order is effective immediately and can be put in place at any time after the cheque is written and up until the day the cheque is presented.

The message from these stories is that bank cheques are not as good as most people think they are. But they are still more reliable than a personal cheque. And due to the sheer security of a cheque, bank cheques may be preferable to cash.

At the very least, as in the cases of Anthony and Mrs J, it should never be assumed that you can get immediate value for a bank cheque.

Alternatives for paying bills

There are big increases in the number of bills that can be paid using a credit card. Provided you use your credit card with care, this is the easiest, most convenient option when it comes to paying bills — even at the cost of a 25-cent telephone call!

Many bills can now be paid at your local post office — telephone, electricity, some council and water rates, and some insurance bills as well. Real estate agents are now issuing swipe cards for tenants to use at post offices in order to pay their rent.

GiroPost is a service which allows customers holding accounts with participating banks and financial institutions to undertake a variety of financial transactions at the post office using credit and ATM cards. You can make deposits, withdrawals or enquires about your account balance, open new accounts and pay monthly credit card bills.

Bedside banking: beating the bank queues

'I prefer to do all my banking in my pyjamas,' says Julie. 'I transferred $2000 into my St George term investment account before breakfast this morning: I knew it started to earn interest from the moment I hung up the phone.'

'I never have to walk into a branch during banking hours — I use the ATM for cash, and have my salary banked direct into my transaction account. It feels good to bank this way.'

While it is not yet clear whether people like Julie are doing virtually all their banking this way, or whether they are simply using it as a convenient extra facility, it is offering many — especially young, busy people — a new way of doing their banking business.

St George claims to handle more than 2 million calls a year for this service.

With most phone banking services, you just dial the number you've been given by the bank and within seconds you are connected to an operator or a computer voice who will guide you through your transaction.

Telephone banking can do the following:

- obtain account balances (including loan accounts)
- check the last 5 transactions on your savings accounts
- transfer funds from selected savings accounts to any other account
- make enquires about other products
- order a statement
- find out interest earned on your accounts last financial year
- pay the bills: these include electricity, telephone accounts, water rates, gas bills and personal loans, as well as a number of department stores, insurance and health insurance companies.

ATMs: no more bank queues!

Go to the Big Fresh supermarket in Gosford, north of Sydney, on a Saturday and not only can you access a Commonwealth Bank ATM to get or deposit cash, but you can touch a screen to get information about bank products or the latest interest rates. Like McDonald's is to food — service and convenience — ATMs are now to banking.

ATMs enable you to withdraw and deposit money outside banking hours, mostly at any time of the day or night. As well you can transfer funds between different accounts and get a cash advance against your credit card. All you need is that plastic card with a magnetic strip on the back and a Personal Identification Number (PIN).

Most bank accounts not only give you ATM access but also make it possible for you to use the expanding Eftpos (Electronic Funds Transfer/Point of Sale) system. This allows you to pay a bill at a range of major retailers by using the same plastic card and PIN that operates the ATM network. When you use this facility money is transferred electronically from your account to the retailer. As a result the card acts as a debit card rather than a credit card.

Now, like the ATM at Gosford, banks are opening mini branches in shopping malls and supermarkets. People will be able to deposit cash in self-service terminals and have the funds immediately credited to their accounts.

The new world of banking has arrived. No more queues!

Still, many of us are so horrified at the thought of never seeing our money again that we simply refuse to use the ATM as a deposit facility!

ATM battles

I'm told that there are more ATMs per head in Australia with more transactions per head than that great consumer society, the USA. So, it comes as no surprise to hear of the countless stories of customers' battles with ATMs. There was even a report several years ago of a Newcastle man attacking an ATM with a sawn-off shotgun. And here is my own story of the *other* side of the ubiquitous ATM.

One Saturday morning my card was swallowed by my branch ATM — with an electronic message telling me that it had expired (I wasn't sure if that meant died or was out of date). I went into the branch the following Monday morning and was informed that my card had indeed expired and that a new card was on its way — 'in about a week or so'.

'But why doesn't the system advise me that my card is due

to expire, so that I can avoid this inconvenience?'

'Sir, the system works by triggering a new card when your old one is returned.'

'But this means that many people have their cards swallowed and are left high and dry.'

'I guess that can happen.' The teller had turned crimson.

OK. Lesson learned. But do you think my card arrived a week later? No. And on my return to the branch, a more senior teller attended my inquiry. This time he keyed a few instructions into his computer and smiled. 'Now you will receive your new card in the post within four days.'

'That's what your colleague told me eight days ago.'

'I'm sorry sir, but things sometimes go awry with cards in the mail.'

'But how do I know that it really will come this time?'

'If it doesn't we'll happily cancel the old card and issue you with a new one.' The teller was still smiling.

All I ask is to have access to my own money and to be treated expeditiously when the bank fails me.

Some tips for effective ATM management:

- Use your bank's ATM for withdrawal; other banks will pass the charges on to you.
- Keep all ATM transaction receipt slips to check against your statement. Include any debits if they are from your cheque book account.
- While some banks have dropped account-keeping fees you may still be paying for ATM use — ranging from 25 to 65 cents per transaction. If you're still paying too much in fees, you may need to cut down on transactions. Keep within the prescribed minimum number of free transactions each month and ensure the account balance is kept above the minimum level required.

- Try to restrict cash withdrawals to one or two each month. If you don't like carrying large amounts of cash, withdraw extra cash through your Eftpos at the supermarket when you pay for your goods.
- When opening an account with a new financial institution look for the location of convenient ATMs.

Banking loyalty: does it matter?

Beryl knew her bank managers well. She had seen a dozen or more move through the chair at her local Commonwealth Bank branch and she always made a point of meeting every new one.

'My father had taught me that if you held a good relationship with your bank manager he was more likely to "bend the rules" for you. You know, call when you accidentally overdrew ... special clearances on cheques ... unusual requests. That kind of thing ...

'So I always make sure that I have a healthy balance in my account. That way I know he'll be pleased with me.'

Such personal relationships with bankers *can* be useful. However, this is probably restricted to the very wealthy and some people in business. Such people *can* derive significant benefit from what is commonly referred to today as *private banking*.

These benefits may include direct access to the bank's investment management people, who may be able to offer individual investment advice. Or, it could be useful for special purposes such as foreign exchange transactions, where the manager could arrange for any transactions to be handled on behalf of the client.

It is, however, highly questionable whether Beryl — or anybody else — is deriving any real benefit from her relationship with the bank manger. Despite a welcoming hand from him or her it is unlikely that he or she would offer Beryl anything that is not currently available to other, more anonymous customers. And, while Beryl's way of conducting her banking gladdens her, it is probable that, in fact, it is costing her real dollars to maintain this *special* — if not archaic — relationship with her bank.

Beryl would be much better off spending her time on the phone checking out opportunities where her funds can yield the greatest benefits.

It would only be good luck, rather than good management, if her bank manager, needing to tie-in the bank's products with Beryl's accounts, will be competitive with other institutions' offerings. What is certain is that Beryl's bank manager's welcoming arms have more to do with the large balance in her account — cheap funds for the bank — than a desire to protect her capital.

At what price loyalty? Rewards for loyal customers are not part of a bank's normal agenda. Look what happened in November last year when the Reserve Bank announced a half per cent rate cut: National Australia Bank, for example, cut its home rates on November 6. But if you were a *loyal* customer of the bank you would not have received your rate cut until December 30.

A number of banks do however offer 'rewards' in the form of discounts on new home loans. St George Bank offers loyal customers a discount of 0.35 per cent off their standard variable home loan rate if they have been with them for five years or more.

For most of us the challenge is more mundane; it's to avoid unnecessary banking costs, to be able to get cash when we need it, and to find the right account for our particular needs.

Tip-offs to rip-offs

- Work out your banking habits and needs: how often you deposit, withdraw, use ATM's or Eftpos etc.
- Select a transactions account that suits your style. Ask your bank for a fee-free or *no-frills* account. Keep within the limits of the number of free transactions. Remember that transactions cover all activities. And watch out for those one-off charges.
- Look at alternatives to bank savings accounts. Try credit unions or cash management trusts.
- Throw away the cheque book! (Well almost!) You can pay bills by:

  — direct debits

  — telephone banking

  — credit card

  — cash, or

  — at the post office (selected accounts only).

Chapter 6

The first battleground: your mortgage

John Symond can hardly wipe the smile from his face these days, even if he tried. John is head of Aussie Home Loans, a lender to home buyers and quite a phenomenon in the industry. He is a classic self-proclaimed example of challenging the big banks and beating them. And, as profits roll John's way, he has also paved the way for all home borrowers to get a better deal from the banks.

There is little doubt that the recent interest rate war between the banks has been sparked not so much by competition between the banks themselves, but by the banks trying to offset the success of the new breed of lenders — mortgage originators such as Aussie Home Loans and RAMS.

But have the banks really changed their spots? With real competition comes choice and lower prices — all to the advantage of the consumer. Yet with competition also comes confusion. *Which loan to choose and which options? And should I switch out of my existing loan? What are the fees involved in switching, and are there hidden costs?*

As I mentioned in Chapter 2 some banks are more competitive than others and this fact is no more important than for your biggest investment — your home. The following sections will give you a better understanding of the mortgage market, what you really need in a home loan and how to select the best loan at the best price.

Dangers for the unwary still exist. Horror stories still abound of people who have over-committed because they were seduced into cheap deals by the banks. And banks have been known to hide the truth — either for short-term gain for the bank or because they don't inform properly.

A whole new code — the Consumer Credit Code — had to be designed to protect unwitting consumers from some of the less than scrupulous practices of lenders. Lenders that include the banks. Now, thanks to the code, anyone taking out a home loan must be given full disclosure of all terms and conditions, the fees and charges that apply, and those that may apply under various circumstances. Lenders now face prosecution if they breach the code.

Yet, despite intense rivalry in the industry not all banks meet the competition. Quotes obtained for a $100 000, 25-year, variable rate home loan ranged from $950 to a $732 in monthly repayments. True, there are many different options in between, but that's still more than a $218 difference — a massive $65 400 over the life of the loan. It would take a lot of bells and whistles to justify that extra cost!

And while the banks were quick to pass on last November's official interest rate cut to new home buyers they have been relatively slow to pass the lower cost of money on to existing home mortgagees. In a truly competitive market the banks would have been forced to cut their lending rates immediately.

There are always traps:

Henry and Alicia received a letter of offer from the bank for their home loan. The interest rate stated on the letter was '8.75 per cent indicative'. The rate was to be fixed for three years.

On settlement of the loan an interest rate of 10.25 per cent was applied for the three years. When Henry and Alicia signed the loan documentation they understood the interest rate would be fixed at 8.75 per cent and claimed they were not made aware that this rate could change.

The loan officer claimed that at the initial interview it was explained that the rate quoted was indicative only and that a different rate may apply at settlement.

There is a very significant difference between 8.75 per cent indicative and 10.25 per cent. Who do you believe?

Remember the bad old days when you had to demonstrate loyalty to a bank before you could apply for a home loan? And the fear and apprehension over waiting for the bank to decide whether you were worthy of being lent their money. Then came the signing process and the costs, often hidden and leaving you hundreds of dollars worse off than you expected.

Today we are almost seduced into taking out the latest home loan, complete with options we don't even understand, from your *very* friendly bank. To compete banks are now even prepared to come direct to the consumer.

Despite improved times in the mortgage market there remain some serious questions that the banks need to answer.

Consider John's experience. This example comes from the Ombudsman's 1995 annual report (name changed).

John had approached his bank in response to a fee-free loan promotion. Although John had not yet found a house, the bank reviewed his application and provisionally approved it subject to inspection of the house when found.

Shortly after submitting his application John moved interstate and found a suitable property in the new location. John approached the bank branch and told the local bank staff of his provisional approval.

The loan was approved and arrangements made for settlement. When John received the Letter of Offer he noticed that the bank had charged him an application fee of $400. He complained to the bank, explaining that he took out the loan on the basis of the fee-free promotion.

The bank considered his claim but advised that the fee-free promotion had ended. The bank offered him $150 on a without prejudice basis in settlement of his complaint.

The bank denied that John had a claim, stating that John's formal application was lodged some time after the expiry of the fee-free promotion. The bank also argued that the Letter of Offer made it clear that fees were payable.

Doesn't this make your blood boil?

It was subsequently found that the bank led John to believe that finance was approved on a fee-free basis and did not advise John that there was an expiry date attached to that offer. After discussions with the Office of the Ombudsman, the bank reassessed John's complaint and waived the fee. John accepted the bank's offer.

Understanding the home loan market

Those of us paying off home loans have seen our repayments slashed over the past few years. Meanwhile new home buyers have not seen rates like this since the early 1970s. We'll now take a look at some important issues such as how much can you really afford and what are some of the pitfalls to watch out for when marketers are chasing your business.

Interest rates halved over the period March 1990 to 1993, creating ideal conditions for what has become the greatest competitive war ever seen in the banking industry. The spawning of mortgage originators such as Aussie Home Loans and RAMS turned banking on its head. Whereas a few years ago most home loans were changed over approximately every seven years, today the amount of *churning* (people switching loans) has increased markedly.

Aggressive competition, however, brings its own problems.

Mr and Mrs C alleged that that the bank should not have approved a five-year fixed rate loan to them because the monthly repayments were unreasonable given their financial circumstances.

The bank stated that at the time of Mr and Mrs C's application it's lending policy was to assess a borrower's repayment capacity based on 35 per cent of their total gross income. The bank acknowledged that Mr and Mrs C's repayments exceeded this amount. However, this was discussed at the time of the application with Mr and Mrs C and they were comfortable with the repayment required.

Because appropriate security was provided and a good savings record was demonstrated, the bank was willing to provide finance as requested. Mr and Mrs C did not dispute the amount of the repayments at the time the loan terms and conditions were signed. It was only when Mr C unexpectedly ceased employment that the issue was raised.

This case went before the Banking Ombudsman who determined that there was no breach of good banking practice in the bank's decision to grant the loan. The Ombudsman's own report made a general observation: 'Consumers continue to complain that the bank should not have granted or approved a loan in the first place.'

Are the banks to blame?

It should be very useful to know where people get into difficulties with their home loans. This section details some of the complaints and problems people have experienced.

The Ombudsman's report detailed some disturbing statistics overall, including that more than 28 per cent of all complaints concerned housing finance. The report stated that the main issues of concern were the:

- accuracy of advertised rates and information provided on front-end fees
- banks' authority to charge fees and deduct funds to meet them
- lack of borrower flexibility and changes to loan conditions, and difficulties experienced by the borrower in terminating loans during the specified loan period.

Even in a competitive environment consumers are provided little relief from the complex loan documentation. Consumers still do not have an adequate understanding of their rights and obligations when entering into a loan contract. The array of options now available has created difficulties for some borrowers in assessing and understanding the particular features offered.

Peter Kell from the Australian Consumers' Association (ACA) says that most people only rely on the advertised interest rates and do not know what they are really paying the banks. 'Even with the new consumer code in place banks are still promoting headline rates which mask the real cost. With full disclosure it is now up to the consumer to read everything and ask the right questions. People will still get into difficulties.'

So-called honeymoon rates have been a notable source of

confusion. A recent report from the ACA found that the average rate paid by borrowers was as low as 7.65 per cent but worked out costing more than 9 per cent per annum over the life of a mortgage.

And if you think you were alone in the confusion surrounding so-called *honeymoon* loans — you're not. Bank customers' gripes about honeymoon rates and variable rate home loans make up the majority of all consumer complaints about banks and bank products.

'It takes a degree in finance to work out the real cost of honeymoon rates. Banks now need to calculate and clearly publicise the annual average percentage rate on their material,' Kell pointed out on this issue.

A new 'comparison rate' will reduce all the cost items to a single figure and provide a meaningful basis for comparing one bank's product with another.

Mr Colin Neave, the Banking Industry Ombudsman, said a large proportion of the home loan complaints arose after 'honeymoon' rates on loans converted back to the variable rate. Often consumers felt they were paying excessively high variable rates and harsh penalties when early termination occurred.

Typically, low introductory rates are available for the first year of a home loan on the condition that the borrower agrees to pay the standard variable rate for a period of three to five years after the *honeymoon* (period) is over.

The banks argue that penalties need to be imposed for early exit because too many people were *churning*. That is, they were taking out 'honeymoon' loans and then switching to another lender at the end of the honeymoon period. Now, under the code, the banks will have to substantiate the costs they are seeking to recover through the application of penalties.

(No doubt a fair number of complaints to the Ombudsman's office were from disgruntled borrowers who thought they could skip from one honeymoon to another.)

Tips

Rising income to cope with rising repayments. Where there is any likelihood of a steady or declining income then *cheap* introductory loans should be avoided. Most borrowers push themselves to their financial limits when they buy a home — especially their first one — and the possibility of rate hikes taking introductory rates to unaffordable levels looms large.

These sort of loans are far more suitable for people who would progressively improve their income — and not necessarily those for whom they are pitched at. Typically, young professionals could consider this type of loan. Another group who could benefit is a couple where one partner is not currently earning an income but who intends to return to the work force thus assisting in servicing this type of loan.

If you are thinking of taking out an introductory loan make sure you check out the lender's standard variable rate and fixed rate mortgages since once the capped period has passed you will need to transfer to one of these options. Make sure they are competitive in the market.

Remember: such loans are mainly used as promotional offers by the banks to attract new customers.

Staying out of trouble

Apart from careful shopping (see pages 132–4 for a list of the types of loans available) and an analysis of what you really need, the most critical question of all is *how much can you afford to borrow*?

The combination of cheap introductory offers, mobile lending and dual incomes provides a potentially deadly cocktail for over-commitment.

There are ground rules. In the case of Mr and Mrs C (see page 111) the rules did not provide an adequate safety net. The 35 per cent rule is one. Another is how we compare to the national average; that is, on the ratio of monthly repayments to monthly take-home pay.

Throughout 1996 this figure slid, starting the year at around 22 per cent and falling to around 19 per cent by December. The fall reflected the lower level of monthly repayments as a direct result of falling mortgage interest rates. (Remember these figures are based on population averages and therefore tend to be biased towards the bulk of the population who have mortgages of between $75 000 and $120 000.)

No one likes to be a statistic, but common sense suggests that if your home loan repayments greatly exceed the norm then either you need to be earning well above average incomes or expecting a rapid rise in the family income.

In any case, some certainty of being able to maintain affordability is the key. A loss of one of the incomes (if there are two incomes in the family) should obviously form an integral part of the calculation. And remember, the risk is not only restricted to a loss of income, it must also include the real (if not certain) possibility that interest rates will rise during the term of the loan.

There are no loan products available which will guarantee a fixed interest rate for the full term of the loan. In fact very few are prepared to fix rates beyond five years. So, if recent history is anything to go by, rates could rise significantly over the average term of a loan.

Tips on managing repayments

- Use a rule of thumb that for an average $100 000, 25-year loan, every percentage point rise in interest rates means an extra $70 a month in monthly repayments.
- Ask your bank to give you a monthly repayment figure for an interest rate 2 per cent higher than the standard variable rate they have on offer, and repeat for 4 per cent higher. It will make for a good reality check.

- Don't go past the maximum percentage of valuation lent: most lenders will require mortgage insurance. The percentage is usually 65 to 85 per cent.
- Deduct $30 000 off your (or combined) income and calculate what effect this has on your cash flow. Can you still service your home loan? Welcome to the real world!
- If you are fully stretched on repayments, and are a two-income family, consider some disability or similar insurance to cover you in the event of loss of one income due to misadventure.

The mortgage maze: features or frills to look for

What have the following got in common: Viridiam, Optimiser, Transformer and Darth Vader? No, they're not all characters from another space epic. But Darth Vader may in fact be in good company with the first three, all of which are products offered by banks and non-banks in the furious war that is being fought for your mortgage dollar.

And if they all give you a feeling that dark forces may indeed be operating, you are probably right. So how are we to deal with the mortgage maze? First, let's look at the general features in a home loan:

Flexible repayments allow the borrower to pay monthly, fortnightly or weekly to suit their own cash flow patterns. Fortnightly (and to a lesser extent, weekly) repayments help repay a loan more quickly as interest on loans is charged on the daily balance. Also, if you divide your monthly by two, for example, and pay fortnightly you will be making one extra repayment per year which will be deducted from the principal (see Chapter 8).

Redraw facilities allow you to make advance payments and then re-use those payments at a later stage if required.

Mortgage offset account: Instead of paying the mortgage (in after-tax dollars) and then having any savings or spare cash in a (taxable) interest-bearing deposit account, the interest on the deposit is not paid but offset against the mortgage. Note that very few banks will give 100 per cent offset. For example, they may charge you 9.0 per cent on the mortgage, but only pay 5 per cent on the deposit.

Loan portability allows you to sell one home and transfer the mortgage to a new one without penalties or new application fees. Again, take care, because this normally requires the loan amounts to be the same (in order to be exempt from fees).

Loyalty discounts: Started by St George, and now provided by a growing list of financial institutions including the Western Australian regional BankWest, these offer customers of five years or more a discount of up to 0.35 per cent off their interest rate on standard variable loans. Other benefits can include annual fee-free credit cards.

Mortgage insurance: Depending on the lender and the percentage of the value of the house you are borrowing, you may be required to take out mortgage insurance. This protects the lender in the event that you default on the loan. It does not protect the borrower. Usually cuts in at around 80 per cent of valuation. It can be very costly, often about 1 per cent of the loan.

Tip: Some lenders charge fees for withdrawals on redraw facilities and account-keeping fees for offset accounts. See pages 134–5 for a full list of fees.

What do you really need in a home loan?

Buyers spend enough time looking for the right house. It makes sense to find a mortgage that suits them too. Despite intense promotion of *cheap* loans, most borrowers opt for a standard variable rate loan, complete with extras. *Here we'll cut through some of the marketing hype and look at what you really need in a home loan.*

Why people prefer the more expensive variable loan to the no frills variety is because of the facilities that come with it: the earlier payment option, redraw, offset, variable repayment schedules, fixed-variable splits and variable to fixed switches. The list goes on.

And while borrowers believe they need these extra features, the truth is that they will never use most of them and therefore are paying for features they don't need.

What is essential for most borrowers and what is really the most valuable feature is *to have the option of putting spare cash into the mortgage and the ability to pay off the loan as quickly as possible.* It is only natural to expect that if you put all your spare money into the mortgage you may need to redraw part of it.

The fact is that few do redraw, with banks reporting a very low rate of redraw. Some saying that redraw usage runs as low as 5 per cent. The other option is to have an *offset* account.

After their wedding Philip and Nicole Zalenik began to look seriously at the property market. And unlike many prospective borrowers who take out a loan by going directly to the bank where they keep most of their accounts, the couple set up stringent criteria to ensure they received the best loan possible.

Their shopping list — you might say — makes sense given the noisy and cluttered market we're in at the moment, with loads of information provided by all participants. With such a range of home loans available on the market, the terms and conditions become a blur of fine print when comparing loans.

And who has the time after all? In all probability many home loans come loaded with features or offer a low interest rate, but seldom do you find these two desirable aspects combined in the one loan.

The Zaleniks approached several institutions, including Westpac and Aussie, with a firm picture in their mind of what they required from a loan: low fees over the full term of the loan and flexibility for a shorter repayment period. A Westpac branch manager showed them different loan scenarios by comparing different repayment terms.

'We wanted something simple, straightforward and with a competitive interest rate. Additional features or options didn't interest us,' said Philip. The couple found that several banks initially fitted their requirements, waiving the establishment fee to make entry into the loan more cost effective.

After looking at the various combinations of home loans on offer, including a standard variable loan, a fixed loan and a combination of the two, the couple tentatively agreed on the Westpac Basic Option home loan. It carried a variable rate of 8.95 per cent, but its features are less flexible than a standard variable home loan, with restrictions on the frequency of repayments.

'Even when we did go to Westpac we didn't decide on the basic home loan straight away,' Philip admitted. 'We made sure we compared it to the deals offered by all the financial institutions we had approached.'

After their house hunting ended with the right house in the eastern suburbs of Melbourne, and despite already comparing a range of bank home loan deals, the couple continued to approach banks with questions. Armed with these answers, the couple matched details with previous loan scenarios, usually using the various banks' telephone inquiry services for information.

But a surprise came late in the proceedings. Philip and Nicole discovered that Westpac had introduced an $8 per month loan administration/account-keeping fee. 'This blew them out of the water as far as we were concerned. We went back to Aussie,' Philip recalled.

At Aussie Home Loans, the couple opted for the no frills variable loan at 8.65 per cent. 'We knew that once a loan was arranged with Aussie there were no more fees or charges. We were prepared to live with some of the slight differences in flexibility. The only disadvantage we found were the delays in getting valuations done.

'Overall we found it helpful to keep a detailed table of information which compared all the different types of loans we'd looked at,' Philip concluded.

This approach to working through the mortgage maze gave them a good sense of accomplishment for a job well done.

While the Aussie loan did not offer all the 'bells and whistles' that other bank loan products may have offered, what the Zalenik story shows is that a sensible and objective approach, based on what was *needed* rather than what was available, showed the way.

What they did give up, for example, were differences in redraw facilities and additional repayment variations. At Westpac, for example, redraws could be arranged over the counter with a minimum redraw of $50. Aussie customers had to apply in writing for approval from the loan trustee and had to draw down a minimum of $5000.

As far as additional payments are concerned, Westpac customers, for example, who wanted to make additional repayments could arrange them in a branch, while Aussie Home Loan customers had to mail a cheque to a post office box in Parramatta, Sydney, and wait 48 hours for the amount to be credited.

Meanwhile, a calculation of the cost to the borrower of the $8 monthly loan administration fee, if capitalised over the full period of the loan, added $2500 to the amount when calculated over 25 years, adding an effective 0.1 per cent to the quoted rate.

Tip: Compile your own table in which you consider the features that are important to you and the details of the various institutions against the relevant feature. To illustrate:

	Institution			
Loan feature of importance to you	**A**	**B**	**C**	**D**
1 Redraw facially	yes	no	yes	yes
2 Offset account	yes	yes	yes	no
3 Flexible repayments	no	yes	no	yes
4				
5 etc.				
6				

The case for fixed rate home loans

Fixed interest rate loans have been overshadowed recently by competition in the market place. But fixed interest loans have traditionally attracted a strong following, particularly with borrowers who follow the market (in interest rates) closely. If interest rates look set to rise, then surely locking in a two to five year fixed rate can provide borrowers with a great advantage?

In this section we'll outline the case for and against fixed interest loans.

Joe and Ellen Tobias took out a loan in the late 1980s when interest rates were much higher than they are at present. Their loan of $120 000 was negotiated at a time when prevailing rates were fluctuating between 15 and 18 per cent for fixed and variable loans, and while these rates seem extraordinarily high at the moment, it was a sad irony at the time that these high interest rates created an air of great uncertainty about which way rates were going.

Joe and Ellen locked themselves into a 17 per cent fixed home loan on the advice of their bank. Monthly repayments of $1800 kept them in financial purgatory for nearly four years until they relieved their suffering by selling their home and paying out their loan.

But not before the bank hit them with an exit fee of nearly $1000, despite having already collected more than $75 000 in interest over the four years.

This horror story presents as a vivid reminder that, while high interest times may have abated, *locking-in* fixed rates require careful consideration. In stark contrast to the crazy 1980s, five-year fixed rates now stand at below 9.0 per cent.

Unfortunately, being able to predict how rates will move is beyond most people. Variable loans follow fluctuations in interest rates. They might be higher than rates fixed a year previously or they might be lower. So choosing when to lock into a rate takes time and confidence. About 20 per cent of borrowers are going for fixed rate loans, as are investment property buyers who need to be able to accurately assess cash flow.

'I hate the roller-coaster of variable rates. I only ever take out fixed loans,' said Paul.

'I took out the first one (fixed loan) because our income was about to be chopped as baby was coming along, and the fixed rate was affordable. Most importantly we didn't have to worry about rates going up for three years.

'A few sums showed us that even though the fixed rate was a little higher than the variable we were paying only $20 a week more.

It was cheap for the peace of mind. It's important not to fix for more than three years. You just can't predict how your life may look in five years.'

Some lenders will not allow advance repayments in fixed loans without hefty penalties. Check whether your lender will allow you to make advance repayments. This is very important to consider and may count as a negative factor against taking out a fixed loan. Chapter 8 explains how large sums of money can be saved by paying off mortgages early through advanced repayments. So consider this when making your decision.

Some argue that a *split loan* is an answer to the problem. But is it?

The decision to split requires an assessment of interest rate trends and then some decision about the proportional split. This is a process requiring too many decisions for most people to bother with. And remember you won't get any meaningful advice from the bank about which way interest rates are going. They don't know!

A check list of your needs

- Do you want the certainty of knowing your regular repayment amount won't change?
- Do you intend to pay more than the required regular minimum monthly repayment amount?
- Understand your situation. Can you afford higher repayments if rates rise in the future? If not, consider a fixed rate loan, or a variation of the period of the loan should rates change.
- Work out how long you are likely to have the loan for. If you think you will repay — or refinance — the loan early watch for early repayment penalties.
- Have a view on interest rates. Will they go up or down? If you think rates will come down let your rate float; that is, the variable rate. If you think rates could rise, consider locking in.

- Obtain written quotes (at least four) before final selection.
- Look closely at all the facilities on offer in the loan: redraw, prepayment, fixed-variable split, etc. Which ones do you really need? Try the *basic* or *no frills* as a starting point with prepayment option only.
- Note that the savings you make on your mortgage are real, after-tax dollars. The right mortgage at the right price can save you money.

What's negotiable

This is 1997. The number of lenders bidding for a share of the market has never been greater.

Being a buyers' market it's natural, therefore, not only to shop around but also to be prepared to negotiate. Some things simply aren't negotiable, but it's possible to sit down and negotiate a better deal when borrowing money or renegotiating an existing loan. Here are some pointers:

1. *Know what you can afford:* Prepare a budget, don't rely on percentage calculations of your gross income. The bank may limit you to a certain percentage but if you have well-prepared documentation you could negotiate a better deal.
2. *Know the market:* Get comparative rates from a number of lending institutions. Be careful to get comparable rates; that is, standard variable against standard variable and not fixed versus variable. Also be careful to get the comparison rate; that is, the rate which takes into account establishment and ongoing fees.
3. *Interest rates:* It is unlikely that the advertised rate of the lender is negotiable. But it is useful to ask for the cheapest rate on offer. That way the lender may come up with another product which meets your needs at a lower rate.

For existing loans, ask for a better rate if your homework suggests you are paying over the odds.

4 *Establishment (application) fees:* Many banks are waiving establishment fees. It is definitely a negotiating point. A reduction in fees at least should be negotiated.

5 *Exit penalties:* These are applicable mainly in fixed term or cheap introductory loans. The same lender may be willing to negotiate if you are seeking a changeover of properties.

Tip: Some banks will offer loyalty discounts to some customers. These translate to a discount of up to 0.35 per cent and fee-free deals on transactions accounts. Also some banks offer discounts of up to 0.5 per cent to members of some professional associations.

Common mistakes

1 *Poor communication:* Poor communication between banks and consumers is a problem for borrowers of variable rate loans, in particular when the interest rates increased in line with market rates. Some borrowers are not being notified of the option, for example, to choose between increasing the loan repayment or extending the loan term. Often borrowers are placing their faith and trust in the bank.

2 *Not reading the fine print:* When it comes to contracts, too many people don't read the small print. And it's the small print that usually contains the bad news. Such provisions may contain penalties that are otherwise not known to you. Whatever the case, sooner or later it could cost you money.

3 *Not locking in a great rate:* Most mortgages now allow a conversion option which allows you to lock in a fixed interest rate. When is conversion to your advantage?

There is no *correct* answer but it makes sense to convert after a sustained period of interest rate falls, similar to what we have seen over the last nine months or so. Check where rates have come from and make a judgement. Look at what's on offer for a 3-year-fixed loan and get a quote on repayments and compare that to your current figure. You may be surprised at how small the difference is.

4 *Using bridging finance:* Buying the second home requires all the skills of a circus performer. It's a daunting task to buy a home without access to the funds from the sale of your current home. Will your bank support you through the turbulent waters of co-ordinating both the sale and purchase of your new home?

But, on the other hand, how can we commit ourselves to a new home without knowing exactly what our home will sell for? And if we want that certainty, who wants to live out of a suit case until you buy that second home. Bridging finance can offer a solution to the above dilemmas — but does it?

Bridging finance

Bridging finance is a loan facility which allows you to fund the purchase of your new home while your present home remains unsold. Effectively it allows you to *own* two homes at once.

But, as is the case with any property-related purchase, banks and other lending institutions will require the same tests as for any *normal* home equity loan. Hence, not only a maximum percentage of valuation, but also the perennial question: '*How much can you afford to pay*?'

This type of finance can't be assumed to be readily available. Another issue is cost. Despite rates being much the same as ordinary mortgage rates, the bridging finance loan carries its own risks.

The Lewis family, like many others, had grown out of their first home — a small semi-detached house in Sydney's inner western suburbs. With their second child on the way, they set their hearts on a new three-bedroom house in Campbelltown, south-west of Sydney.

Their real estate agent recommended a sale price of $185 000 for their semi, but he was confident of getting more. Meanwhile they secured their Campbelltown house at auction for $245 000, having saved the $25 000 they needed for the 10 per cent deposit.

It came as a shock to the Lewises that no one bid for their property at the auction the following Saturday. By mid-week one couple had approached the real estate agent with an offer of $165 000. The Lewises declined the offer and waited.

Settlement dates were looming and they knew they were locked in. Not wanting to lose their deposit, the Lewises went cap-in-hand to their bank, seeking a bridging loan on the new property. All up, they needed $235 000, taking into account stamp duty and legal costs.

The bank assessed that they were in a position to take out a bridging loan if they could come up with another $25 000! After some begging and pleading with family members, they raised the money and secured the bridging loan.

The bank insisted that it be cleared within 120 days. They also insisted on an establishment fee of $700 and offered the funds: $210 000 at a fixed rate of 9.5 per cent, interest only. The following month they were up for $5212. This comprised:

One month's interest plus establishment fee (new loan)	$2362
Existing mortgage repayment	$950
Mortgage insurance	$1900

The nightmare had begun.

They had only budgeted for repayments of a maximum of $1200 per month and were forced to draw cash advances against their credit card to meet their living expenses.

Five weeks later the Lewises sold their semi for $172 500, and six weeks after that they discharged their bridging loan, paying an additional $400 in exit fees.

The bridging loan had cost the Lewises $7405, made up as follows:

Establishment fees	$700
Interest charges (11 weeks)	$4220
Exit fees	$400
Interest on bankcard ($5000 at 19 per cent for 10 weeks)	$185
Mortgage insurance	$1900

Based on the 11-week term of the loan this equates to an effective interest rate of 16.7 per cent ($7405 on $210 000 for 11 weeks) — nearly 8 percentage points above the average rate of variable home loan interest rates.

The Lewises flush of excitement and lack of planning cost them at least $7400 in additional expenses and gut-wrenching worry. The pressure to sell their semi-detached home was unbearable and they probably lost a few thousand more by having to discount the sale price.

Often bridging finance is not the solution that most people expect. The message is to be wary and not allow the situation to get to the desperate circumstances the Lewis's found themselves in. The only winner in that case was the bank.

Even renting short term would have been a cheaper option, although the best option by far is to be meticulous in planning both the sale and purchase. Many people manage quite well to co-ordinate the settlement of two properties. And certainly a good solicitor will be very helpful in the timing process.

Getting out of your mortgage

Exit fees are the costs you face when getting out of your mortgage. They're complicated, confusing and expensive, and you can only avoid them by careful planning. For many such planning is anathema. The thought of getting out of a mortgage early does not normally come into consideration. But today, in a far more competitive home lending environment than ever before, you could be shooting yourself in the foot by not planning for the possibility of refinancing your home elsewhere.

After all, real rates have fallen 2 per cent or more in the past few years, and if your bank isn't giving you the best possible deal, then switching could be considered. Moreover, with most states abolishing stamp duty payable on refinanced mortgages, switching is a real attraction. But before you consider such a switch read the small print on your current mortgage — look for exit fees, early termination fees or the like.

Due to the many complaints and confusion this issue attracts, the new Consumer Credit Code now places the onus on banks to demonstrate the amount the customer will be out of pocket in an early termination case. Basically the code makes exit penalties illegal beyond the *out-of-pocket* amount. Watch for any excess charge should the situation arise. A number of banks, including Westpac and NAB, have stated that even on introductory loans there would be no exit penalty on contracts entered into after 1 Novemeber 1996.

The solution to the question of avoiding excessive termination payments is to ensure that a Letter of Offer from the bank specifically details any costs for early termination and the express method used to calculate the cost. If there are other costs involved demand a better deal; indicate that you do not wish to pay any other costs.

So is it worth it?

1 Work out the cost of *not* switching

Get a quote for a new loan. Multiply the monthly difference over the full term of the loan. I would be surprised if any exit penalty could stack up against the size of savings potentially available.

2 Ask your bank for a better deal

Then, if you are still considering a switch — and many home borrowers are these days — there is no short cut. You will need to calculate exactly what it will cost to get out of your loan. Then add the expenses of a new loan and include all fees and stamp duty if applicable.

Once you have a firm idea of the costs, calculate the savings on your new loan.

Begin with the first 12 months and look ahead in 12-month increments, until the savings start outweighing the costs. After you have completed the sums you should know whether it is smarter to switch to a cheaper loan.

Alan and Fran ran their own courier business. Fran did all the paper work — both business and personal. Alan is unreserved in his praise: 'She's very together, very organised — more than I've ever been.'

They entered the housing market ten years ago. Interest rates were rising and Alan and Fran found themselves paying up to 18 per cent in interest. As rates began to fall, they made a decision: 'We kept to the same level of repayments and paid off our loan in 8 years.'

Alan and Fran were now in the market for a bigger home, and they started by analysing what they needed in a home loan.

'The most important factor was flexibility. We needed a loan that would account for the financial uncertainties associated with running a business and having two small children.

'Of course a low interest rate was important! 'We approached our bank but found that they weren't flexible enough.

'We were told about a home loan selection service who could help us evaluate a variety of banks and lending institutions so that we could choose the best home loan.

'In the end we decided against a low variable rate; we wanted some protection against interest rate increases.

We liked the suggestion of a loan that was partially variable; this gave us the flexibility of paying the principle off our loan when were able, and it also allowed us to pay interest only if we needed to.

'We placed three-quarters of our loan under a fixed term for three years, with the remaining quarter being a variable loan. Other features which we thought might come in handy in the future included access to additional lines of credit, a redraw facility on the variable portion of the loan, and no fee to refix after the fixed term expires.

'This means we can rethink the loan after our three-year fixed term. One of the reasons we were able to pay off our first loan quickly was because we re-evaluated the loan every three years or so, each time arranging to increase repayments and reducing the term of the loan. It made us feel good to have shopped around with the help of an expert that wasn't a bank pushing its own products.'

Fran offers some other common sense advice: 'Anyone taking out a loan should re-evaluate the loan on a regular basis to investigate ways in which you can reduce its term.'

An explanation of loans and the fees and charges involved

The players

Banks are generally not the cheapest for basic loans but they can offer transaction accounts and offset deposit accounts. They can also offer more flexibility if you need more than just a mortgage; for example, a personal loan which might use the same security as the mortgage.

Mortgage originators raise their funds from either the banks or from the professional money market. They then add a *margin* of anything from 0.6 to 1.5 per cent. Mortgage originators are smaller and can operate on lower margins than banks. Though they don't offer the flexibility of the banks they continuously enhance their products to compete against the banks. Examples of mortgage originators include Aussie Home Loans, RAMS, AMP, MLC, FAI and National Mutual.

Building Societies/Credit Unions link transaction accounts and deposit accounts, giving greater flexibility.

Types of loans

Standard variable loans: the interest rate can vary throughout the term of the loan. These are closely linked to the movement of official (Reserve Bank set) interest rates, although competitive forces have pushed these rates down in the past 12 months beyond official interest rates. The term is usually 20 or 25 years. This is Australia's most popular type of home loan.

Basic variable loan: also referred to as a *no frills* loan. This is similar to the standard variable loan but with less features; for example, it may not offer a redraw facility, flexible payment options or portability.

Fixed rate loan: interest rate and repayments are fixed for a set period, usually between one and five years, with the most popular being two or three years. Most fixed loans will automatically default to a variable loan at the end of the *fixed* term.

Most lenders will allow a rollover into another fixed term. These types of loans are becoming increasingly popular for obvious reasons: certainty in the amount of the repayments and no risk of interest rate hikes during the fixed term.

Honeymoon loans: also referred to as a *low start* loan. Very low rates are charged for the first year (up to two percentage points lower than the standard variable rate). The loan then reverts to the standard variable rate. This was a very popular form of home loan with virtually all banks competing.

Capped loans: these loans have an interest rate ceiling for a fixed period of time. The rate cannot exceed this ceiling during the specified period. Should rates go down the rate you pay may fall below this ceiling. Rates are normally capped for up to one year; they then default to the standard variable rate. Capped loans tend to be identical to the honeymoon rate and are offered only to new customers, not existing loans.

Split loans: a loan that enables borrowers to take up part of their loan as a variable rate loan and as part of a fixed rate loan. This type of loan offers borrowers the ability to hedge their bets. Split loans are popular when interest rates enter into periods of volatility.

Home equity loans: a line of credit which is secured by a mortgage over a residential property. Such loans are often used for extensions and renovations, buying an investment property, or lifestyle purposes such as holidays or overseas travel.

Consolidation loans: a borrower can combine several loans; for example, an existing mortgage, personal overdraft or credit card debts into one single rate loan — all using the home as a security.

Frills

Features portability, redraw facilities and flexible repayments schedules.

Offset accounts: interest earned is offset against mortgage interest. This is not assessable as income earned for tax purposes.

Salary accounts: These are a new version of the home equity loan, and can significantly reduce the interest payable on a loan over time. But watch out for the traps (see Chapter 7).

Fees

Establishment (Application) fees: fees charged on securing the loan. These include valuation reports, preparation of security documents, cost of stamping and registering security documents, and stamp duty on the letter of offer. Many banks and other lenders are currently waiving application fees for new borrowers.

Account keeping or debt administration fee: usually a monthly fee. These fees are usually between $3 and $8 per month. This doesn't sound like much but over the life of the loan it can be a tidy sum.

Switching fee: when a customer lodges an application for part or whole of the outstanding balance to be switched from one type of loan to another (same institution).

Exit fees: costs the borrower faces when getting out of the mortgage. Of particular concern are the fees that are charged when cheap introductory deals are broken at the end of the honeymoon period. Under new consumer code rules this fee needs to be justified by the bank.

Redraw charges: some banks will charge the borrower a fee to withdraw certain funds.

Jargon

Indicative interest rate: the rate indicated at the time of inquiry — not at the time of executing the loan agreement.

Letter of offer: the letter from the bank to the intending borrower setting out the terms and conditions of the loan. The letter of offer can, under certain circumstances, be withdrawn.

Loan default: customers in default of their loan repayments face the prospect of the bank taking legal action to sell their house in order to discharge the loan.

Tip-offs to rip-offs

- Check your existing mortgage repayments against the quoted interest rate: are you paying the correct amount each month?
- When you are shopping ask your bank for the *comparison rate* not just the *headline* interest rate. This places all cost items into a single figure.

- Calculate your own affordability ratio (ratio of repayments to take-home pay) and subtract $30 000 from your combined salary to assess the risk factor.
- All costs should be once-only; that is, paid at the time the home loan is taken out. If a bank tries to add a cost which is ongoing, go elsewhere. An example is a *service fee* which some banks charge on a monthly or yearly basis. The effect is the same as increasing the interest rate. It's a rip-off!
- Obtain in writing the full amount to be provided, the annual percentage interest rate, how the interest is calculated and debited, the total amount of interest if the contract is paid out in seven years, all fees and charges, how you will be advised of any interest rate changes, and how often you will receive a statement.
- Avoid bridging finance. If you can't juggle the two properties, then rent for a while.

Chapter 7

Other loans: cutting the cost of your debts

Kevin, a 23-year old telephone technician, had debts of $18 000, comprising three plastic card debts to three different financiers, including one bank, totalling $4000 (one for $2400 despite a limit of $1500) for a range of goods: stereo equipment, camcorder and even grocery accounts at a department store.

Kevin also had three personal loans — one with a finance company ($5000 for a car loan currently being repaid at the rate of $270 per month) and two with two different banks — one for $5000 and the other for $10 000, with only $4000 balance to pay.

Kevin's repayments for the six banks and finance companies amounted to a total of $1100 a month, or around $275 per week. His living expenses — the basics, for food, car running costs, telephone and food — amounted to $180 per week. His after-tax take-home pay was $395 per week.

He was short by $60 a week and the dogs were out. He already had a debt collection agency — appointed by one of the finance companies — demanding full payment of his debt of $2400. Kevin turned to one of the credit counselling services for help.

Kevin, who admitted to the credit counsellor that he was a credit junkie, was facing bankruptcy. None of his purchases held any of their original value. Even the car, which he needed to commute to and from work, was now worth less than $5000.

The counsellor advised Kevin to opt for bankruptcy, an outcome that would affect him financially for years to come, and at the more profound personal level, make him feel like a failure.

Too much debt is certainly a recipe for disaster, but managing your debts can both get you what you need and keep you out of strife. Most of us seem to get by with a clutch of debts: the home mortgage, credit cards, the car loan and maybe even an overdraft or personal loan. Almost certainly too much interest is being paid and repayments causing unnecessary strains on the budget.

In this chapter, rather than preach *no debt* we'll look at *managing* debt in such a way as to reduce costs overall and to use our personal cash flows more effectively.

A recent Newspoll survey found the main cause of personal stress for 30 per cent of Australians is personal finances. Young people, in particular, are vulnerable. But it's not only young people who lose control of their finances and end up in trouble.

After all, we do live in a society where debt is accepted as a way of life. We owe financial institutions a total of nearly $3500 for every adult (ABS and Reserve Bank figures). And the credit binge continues with recent figures showing that we are indeed a nation of borrowers rather than savers, with household debt soaring by another 12 per cent last year.

'The big concern is that mortgage rates are coming down at a time when household debt is still rising strongly,' said AMP Investments' chief economist Dr Shane Oliver late last year in an interview with the *Sydney Morning Herald*. Dr Oliver said the rate cuts would ease the repayment burden for many borrowers but would also encourage them to borrow more, leaving them vulnerable to shock when rates 'inevitably rose again'.

And if this all seems a bit too removed from your own pocket, read some more basic home truths about cost.

'Many people don't understand the high cost of credit. People don't realise they pay up to 23 per cent interest on credit cards, so the advantages of buying on special are lost.' Ms Deborah Hunter, coordinator for Credit Helpline financial counselling services, says that many of the people she sees aren't even aware of what interest rates they're paying. 'The thing to remember whenever you go into debt is that you create risk for yourself, particularly with long-term debt like a housing loan.

'Generally these people live for the day and tomorrow catches up on them.'

Too many debts does not mean too much debt

For those with the inevitable *clutch* of loans list them and analyse the costs:

Consider Jan's and Tony's debts as an example:

Amount owning on credit cards	$5 000
Balance left to pay on personal loan on motor vehicle	$5 500
Overdraft facility	$3 000
Total	$13 500

Yearly costs associated with these debts:

Interest on credit card (average) @16.95%	$848
Interest payable on personal loan @ 19.9%	$1150
Fee on overdraft facility	$200
Total	$2200

Bank fees and interest charges are absorbing more than $2200 a year — after paying establishment fees of $500 for the two loans. That's a very high price to pay for convenience.

Although simultaneously running a credit card balance that is not out of control, an overdraft facility for *emergencies*, a hire purchase plan for the car and a mortgage that may not appear to be too extravagant to Jan and Tony, it is a gross waste of money. We'll look now at better ways to run these debts.

How to consolidate your debts

By consolidation I mean taking a number of smaller loans and combining them in to one larger short-term loan. This can be achieved by going to your bank and asking for a loan that enables you to eliminate the smaller, more expensive loans with a cheaper loan.

For the purposes of this exercise I suggest excluding the home mortgage as it represents a long-term loan; it is not wise to combine it with a short-term loan.

For simplicity the consumer has two separate loans:

- a mortgage
- other (for car, credit card debts and other expenses that are out of control).

Most banks will consider a consolidation deal, provided it is well thought through and makes sense. Consolidation does make sense when interest rates of 17 per cent or more are being paid on after-tax money when even unsecured money is available at 13 per cent or less. Where security is available (e.g. your home) the rates drop even further, down to under 10 per cent in many cases.

Look at the following analysis of Jan's and Tony's loans:

Debt	Amount ($)	Interest (%)	Monthly payment ($)
Mortgage	90 000	9.5	890
Car loan (balance)	5 500	19.9	250
Visa	2 300	14.75	n/a*
Store card	900	22.0	n/a*
Bankcard	1 800	14.75	n/a*
Overdraft facility	3 000	12.25	n/a*
Total monthly repayments			1640

* *(assume run down over 12 months; monthly repay @ $500)*

Here is an example of what the situation looks like when Jan and Tony consolidated — they borrowed $13 500 from the bank and paid out all their smaller debts.

Debt restructure with a consolidation* loan

Debt	Amount ($)	Interest (%)	Monthly payment ($)
Mortgage	90 000	9.5	890
Consolidation loan; 3-year	13 500	9.5	432

* *assume security of home is provided*

Jan's and Tony's loans, apart from the mortgage, were combined into one three-year consolidation loan. The savings are substantial. Apart from a monthly reduction in repayments of

$320, the consolidation loan over three years meant a total saving in interest payments of $2500.

I have not heard of one bank that has approached any of its customers and suggested this type of consolidation. The reason is simple: it is not in their interest to do so!

There are thus compelling reasons for taking out consolidating loans, but there may be some disadvantages:

- It can be risky using the home as security for a car loan. Should you default on the car loan you wouldn't want to risk the home.
- If the various loans only have short-term repayments left, consolidation will not be as beneficial.

Tips

- Use the bank to your advantage: ask it for a consolidation deal, but insist on a variable rate loan and flexible terms that allow you to pay the loan off earlier.
- Avoid lumping on to the primary mortgage: it doesn't make sense to convert short-term loans into 15- to 25-year loans

The loan maze: how to avoid being ripped off

Interest charges and bank fees do add up and selecting the best loan is not a job for the faint-hearted. But the savings derived by the right choice can be huge. The personal loan market, in particular, is being eroded by home equity loans and credit cards, and the potential benefits arising out of smart shopping are greater than ever. Rates and fees vary enormously — often by more than 4.5 percentage points and $100 or more on fees. *Let's see how you can ensure that you won't get ripped off!*

The main players in personal finance

Banks: Most will offer loan products ranging from overdrafts (secured) to unsecured personal loans. Both variable and fixed rates are on offer. For variable rate loans, watch out for the upfront fees as these can be quite hefty and will alter the comparison interest rate. Rates vary from around 9.25 per cent for a fixed (one-year) loan of up to 15 per cent for an unsecured variable loan. Entry fees range from zero to $350.

Overdraft facility: Such facilities are more useful as a business-related account and can be very expensive, both in terms of establishment fees and ongoing interest rates when compared to other forms of personal loans. And they vary considerably from bank to bank, with some banks charging several per cent over what they refer to as their *base rate*.

Almost all banks will charge a *line fee*, which is a charge for the overdraft facility even if you don't use it. Overdrafts usually require some form of security, and, more often than not, this is in the form of residential property. This would tend to exclude those who are renting.

Credit unions tend to offer the cheapest personal loans, with many tailoring special purpose products at target markets such as the new and used car markets. The Power Credit Union (NSW), for example, offers a car loan at 10.9 per cent and an entry fee of $40. Other credit unions may have no entry fee but a slightly higher interest rate.

A note about credit unions. Credit Unions are not-for-profit organisations. Operating expenses are paid and prudent levels of reserves are set aside, all remaining profits go back to the members through better savings rates, better rates for loans and improved services. While most credit unions provide a range of banking services, one drawback is the fact that many of them don't have the financial resources to lend heavily for housing. However, this doesn't preclude you from using them for your mainstream banking needs since you can go elsewhere for your home loan.

Unlike the banks, which offer a single personal loan product for everything, credit unions have tiered rates. These rates are specific to the *asset* the borrower requires. So, for example, this means that car loans, especially those for new cars, tend to be viewed more favourably than other personal loans. Although credit unions are more difficult to access, with far fewer branches than banks, the great potential advantage that they offer is that, as member-owned cooperatives, credit unions are operated solely for the benefit of their members. Credit unions have a lower fee structure than banks, most of them charging between zero and $100 for personal loans.

As a further illustration of the different tiers, State Government Employees, one of the largest credit unions, has three options: new cars at 12.5 per cent, second-hand cars at 13.3 per cent and personal loans at 15.9 per cent. Community First Credit Union also has a *low* car rate at 10.9 per cent and personal loans rated at 18.25 per cent.

You can avoid the banks for personal loans or specific purpose loans: banks have higher rates and charge an entry fee of about $100. Tailoring your needs to the loan is the answer. For cars (and the like) look to the credit unions. For consolidation loans look to the banks or credit unions.

Need a loan?

Not having equity in a home doesn't mean you have to pay exorbitant interest rates for a loan. There are essential steps in the process of getting the *right* loan:

The first and most important question to ask is: 'Can I afford the repayments without getting out of my depth?'

Second, make at least three comparisons of the rate and fees offered. If you prefer to have the interest rate fixed for the term of the loan in order to be able to budget for the exact amount, then get a personal loan from a bank. If you prefer to have a variable rate loan then credit unions are usually the best.

Here is a list of points to consider:

- What is the term of the loan?
- Is it a fixed rate or is it variable?
- What are the fees and charges incurred in establishing the loan?
- What extra (hidden) costs are there?
- What security or guarantee (if any) do you need to obtain the loan?
- Obtain a written quote detailing all costs and terms of the loan before signing any loan agreement.

A thorough analysis of your case needs to be carried out. However, sometimes a credit card is a better option than a personal loan due the personal loan's high entry fee. There is little to compare between credit cards, personal loans or overdrafts when it comes to small purchases.

The lack of entry fees and the flexibility in repayment makes the credit card the preferred option for small purchases, although the generally higher interest rates make credit cards an expensive form of *loan* on all but the smallest, short-term credit purchases.

Some people are in favour of a specific purpose loan for the purchase of a car. A loan for the life of the car does make sense — paying it off in three to five years. There is some comfort and convenience in knowing how much it is going to cost and how much to budget for. But don't take out a specific purpose loan if you have credit card accounts out of control. With plastic, you recycle debt and never get off the treadmill.

For first-time borrowers

Getting your loan approved: use the bank, but first ...

There is not much point in applying for a loan if you're going to get knocked back. The best way to beat the banks is to give them the least in fees and interest. Getting the right loan under the right conditions will ensure you get the outcome you want. But you need to be aware of how a bank goes about determining whether you are *credit ready*.

When a bank evaluates a loan application it takes into consideration a number of criteria, including:

- serviceability
- type of security offered
- the applicant's asset and liability position, credit history, personal background and character.

These days, you don't have to have a savings record with a bank or building society in order to qualify for a personal or home loan. So for those who want more than to be identified as a pin number at the bank, credit unions represent a viable alternative — here you are a member and an individual.

Your own credit profile

Developing your profile is a foolproof way of getting the loan you need. To do this you need to obtain:

- A letter from your *employer* setting out your terms of employment and, if possible, some glowing endorsement of your value to the organisation.

- A letter from your *bank manager* where you have maintained savings and/or chequing accounts indicating that you have maintained your account in a credit situation (detailing a minimum balance) for at least twelve months. (This will surprise most managers but press on regardless.)
- A list of all your *assets* and *liabilities*. (Don't forget, an anticipated tax refund (if applicable) is considered an asset.)
- A *budget document* which should list all possible expenses you can expect over a twelve-month period. This should be broken down into a cash flow to indicate payments such as insurance and motor vehicle annual charges — include all expenses related to the loan you are considering.
- Have available your *tax file number* and identification papers, such as driver's licence, passport and birth certificate, and a couple of domestic-type bills such as water rates or electricity.

Home equity-based loans

For those with equity in their home, a solution is at hand. Let's examine how you can maximise this to your advantage and obtain *cheap* loans.

The past couple of years have seen the banks clamouring around our front doors with unsolicited invitations to use your equity in your home to raise some extra cash. The story may go something like this: why have the equity you have built up in your home sitting there idly? Why not put it to work by using it to secure new *high performance* loans to enable you to buy shares or an investment property or some other asset? And why pay high personal loan-type interest rates when you can borrow on this equity at interest rates only slightly higher than for the standard home loan?

Who could resist? Taking out a home equity loan is simply taking out a new mortgage on your home. Anyone who has a home loan which accounts for less than 80 per cent of the value of the loan can usually get a home equity loan. And as rates are similar to the standard home lending rates, they are much cheaper than personal loans, at least as far as interest rates are concerned.

However, upfront fees can be steep, similar to home loans, so the comparison against personal loan rates must be made by adding the fees to the interest charges over the duration of the loan.

It would be difficult to justify, for example, paying $600 or $700 in fees to take an equity home loan for a relatively small loan of, say, a few thousand dollars, despite the much lower rate of interest than credit card finance or personal loan finance.

The purpose of home equity-based loans needs careful consideration. It is just too easy to get carried away with the idea of *mortgage power.* There are risks. Surely it follows that bank borrowers who stretch their borrowing's based on today's *low* interest rates may not be capable of servicing that loan when inevitably interest rates rise next year or the year after.

The main attraction of home equity-based loans is that if they are put in place as the primary mortgage, the borrower can use as little or as much of the approved loan amount as he or she wants. As well, he or she can repay this and draw it out again at any time. Such loans are therefore an excellent source of finance for, say, investors wanting quick access to relatively low-cost funds.

The biggest trap of home equity-based loans is the way in which they give a home buyer the ability to *spend* the equity already built up in the family home. This is because the lender is not concerned about the purpose of the loan, merely that the security is bricks-and-mortar and that the repayments can be met.

Let's say you sat down one evening and worked out that the market value of your home was $200 000 and you had $50 000 left to pay on your mortgage. You felt pretty good because that meant you had equity in your home of $150 000 and it was just sitting there. The temptation to buy a new car and to go on that overseas holiday was just too great.

So, you went to your friendly bank and, armed with the knowledge that this equity was available, negotiated a mortgage-backed revolving line of credit — a home equity loan — of $50 000 at a very competitive rate of 9.5 per cent, variable, over 15 years, and with no upfront fees! But rather than pay two sets of repayments you find that you can add to the existing loan of $50 000, resulting in $900 to repay each month.

The additional $520 in repayments each month — $6240 a year — means that you (as an average taxpayer) would have to earn an additional $10 000 or more a year to maintain your current lifestyle. And that's for fifteen years!

You will carry this extra burden for 15 years just to get back to the same home equity you started with. Your ability to borrow has also been reduced against your now diminished equity and higher debt repayment burden, making it very difficult to accumulate enough capital for a significant investment. It seems like a very expensive holiday indeed!

The use of such loans to finance consumption should be handled *very cautiously*. If money is needed for a vacation, there is a case for taking out a personal loan or a credit card loan despite my earlier warnings that these borrowings can get out of hand very easily. This means that you are forced to pay the debt off earlier — say over a couple of years — rather than over a 15- or 25-year mortgage term because the interest rates are high.

The kind of equity loan that offers you a revolving line of credit can easily tempt you to use it irresponsibly for unnecessary or unaffordable goods and services — much as some borrowers use credit cards for high risk activities, such as going into business or investing on the stock market.

The important distinction between home equity debt and credit card or other forms of debt, however, is that the home equity debt exposes your home to foreclosure, whereas other forms of debt do not. If, for example, you have a $50 000 underlying mortgage, and take out a $75 000 home equity loan for the purchase of a business and you default on your repayments because of business problems at a time of severe weakness in the real estate market, foreclosure by the bank and a forced sale may not even yield $125 000. In that case, after the bank is paid off, there is nothing left — and you will be homeless.

Home equity loans can work in reverse and may cost you the best chance for achieving financial independence. They should be used mainly by investors.

Negative gearing

Marilyn owned her home — a unit in Sydney's eastern suburbs — outright, and earned a reasonable income as a manager of a haberdashery shop. As result of a divorce settlement she had some $70 000 parked in a term deposit at the bank. She always complained about the tax she had to pay. She had read about negative gearing and finally after her family encouraged her to do something about it, she went off to her bank manger to arrange a loan.

They worked out that Marilyn would have to make a loss of about $5000 a year to reduce her tax bill by a meaningful degree. She calculated that she would be able to live quite comfortably off her salary less the few thousand that would be needed to service the loan. After confirming the figures with her accountant, she went into the market looking for an investment property with up to $500 000 to spend.

The property Marilyn eventually bought was a small

commercial building in the Sydney industrial suburb of Marrickville — tenanted by a computer printer supplier. The total purchase price came in at $515 000. She had put in $65 000 cash and borrowed the balance — $450 000 — from the bank, putting up the security for both her home unit and the investment property as collateral (at the request of the bank).

The figures looked like this:

Rental income	$46 000
Less	
Agent/manager commission @ 6%	$2760
Rates and taxes	$1500
Repairs and maintenance	$1700
Interest on $450 000	$45 000
Net loss	$5000

This loss will be tax deductable against her other income. This is negative gearing. At a marginal tax rate of 43 cents in the dollar the reduction in tax liability will be:

$5000 × 43 % = $2150

Thus the net after-tax cost to Marilyn will be:

Cash outlaid to fund loss on property	$5000
less Reduction in tax to pay	$2150
Net outlay	$2850

But as in most rental properties tenancy is never guaranteed. Moreover, in commercial tenancies the risk of businesses failing is always a significant factor. In this case the business failed and it took two months of arrears in payments before the premises were vacated. It took another two months to find a new tenant, but a discount of 5 per cent on the rent had to be offered as well as a rent-free period of three months as an inducement.

Bills were mounting and six months after the first signs of trouble from the computer company, Marilyn had accumulated bills relating to the investment property amounting to $2500 — including a $750 legal bill for an eviction notice — and she had run down her savings to nil in order to meet her interest payments.

From a comfortable existence with her only aggravation being her tax assessment, Marilyn's life had become a misery. She had to get out of the property.

She put it on the market with instructions to sell quickly. Eighteen months after her $495 000 purchase she sold the property for $465 000, less agent's commission and solicitor's fees. As she had fixed her loan for three years, Marilyn was required to pay an exit fee of $2600 to the bank.

Her nest egg of $70 000 had shrunk to $1200.

There has never been an easier time for home owners to negative gear. To own shares or investment property. Not only are the banks bidding for that slice of your home equity, but also the credit unions have got into the act. One ad tells the story: 'Use your equity in your home to buy that investment property and at the same time earn yourself another tax deduction.' Another ad reads: 'If you have $50 000 equity in your home we will show you how to become a millionaire.'

It's not my place to advise on matters dealing with any individual's tax circumstances, but I have come across a number of cases of people entering into negative gearing schemes who should never have been there. It seems that some bank marketing people are pushing the story a little indiscriminately. Marilyn's story is a sober reminder of some of the risks of negative gearing.

There is little doubt that there are many, many people who can derive benefits from negative gearing, but there are traps for the unwary. As usual, banks are not the ones to be guiding you through the maze.

The success of products such as Citicorp's *Home Credit* and *Mortgage Power* are indicative of the strong marketing opportunity that the banks are exploiting. And the products coming through are becoming increasingly sophisticated.

In the case of the *Home Credit* product, for example, it is possible to split the loan in two. That is, two loans within the facility: one would be used to pay off the family home and the other to pay for an investment. The strategy is to pay off the home loan portion as quickly as possible and build up equity in an asset that is exempt from capital gains tax.

At the same time the borrower would make no repayments on the investment portion of the loan, allowing interest to be capitalised and higher tax deductions generated.

How many people do you know who have bought that little holiday home up or down the coast as an investment property? You know the concept: *negative gear* — purchase the property, rent it out for most of the year, then use it for your family. Well, in a nutshell, it doesn't work. Not from an investment point of view.

Just drive up and down the coast of NSW, Victoria, or Queensland and you'll find the coastline littered with *for sale* signs and almost bereft of people outside the holiday season. The holiday house that looked like such a reasonable purchase back in the boom-time 1970s and 1980s has turned into a lump of lead around the owners' ankles in the 1990s.

If you are buying it on a home equity loan, you can't expect to negatively gear a holiday home you only rent out for five or six weeks a year. From the taxman's realistic perspective it's not an income-earning proposition, it's a luxury! And with most of the coastline up for sale the prospects of a capital gain are virtually zero. It would be cheaper to fly the family to Aspen, Colorado, for the ski season.

Do people realise just how much time and effort is taken up in managing a property? It isn't just a matter of transferring the hassle to a real estate agent. Not only is the cost substantial but there is no guarantee that the job will be done properly. One of the biggest problems is the difficulty of getting the right tenants: horror stories abound of unreliable and house-destroying tenants.

Apart from that the numbers just don't stack up. The average property investor would need to achieve about a 16 per cent return over, say, five years just to cover buying and selling costs, and the after-tax loss incurred as a result of interest costs exceeding net rental income (negative gearing).

Negative gearing will not work if the property becomes vacant or if the tenant stops paying rent.

There are good reasons why property investors should stop and ask themselves: 'Are all the potential hassles associated with real estate investment justified by the likely returns?' Even in the event of *successful* negative gearing — that is, where a profit is actually struck and tax deductions derived — profits made on the sale of the property are subject to capital gains tax.

Only when investors have asked this question can they make a realistic decision about whether or not negatively gearing into real estate is a better option than, for example, superannuation. There are other risks for the unwitting investor. Your income could drop and you may no longer be able to afford to fund the losses. You may be forced to sell the property in a weak market.

Negative gearing certainly works for the banks. It generate lots of interest and fees backed by bricks-and-mortar security.

During 1992–93 there were plenty of sad stories told around dinner-party tables of people who had purchased negatively geared investment properties during the property boom of the late 1980s only to be squeezed by the massive interest rate hikes of 1990–92 (Keating's recession 'that we had to have').

Many lost not only their investment capital but their homes after being forced to sell by banks who were bleeding profusely from their own massive bad debts after the lending binge to the entrepreneurs.

Even in the absence of such poor economic conditions, negative gearing becomes a direct loss if there is no increase in the value of the property to compensate for the annual shortfall of income over expenses. *Negative gearing will not work if the property market stays flat or declines. Investors will succeed only in paying more interest.*

Borrowing against the security of the house and converting that into a single loan is a double-edged sword. Borrowers should always remember that the loan is secured by a mortgage over the property, and in the case of default the lender would be entitled to sell the house — your family home — to recover his money.

Separating the investment property from your family home with two separate loans affords another layer of protection. It allows you and your family to sleep at nights. The banks will always try to secure as much collateral security as they can, so you need to be firm in your own resolve. But you will need to have both a deposit and the ability to fund the investment property.

Negative gearing on shares

The same principles of negative gearing can apply to shares. You will need to take just as much, if not more care here.

A number of banks have made unsolicited offers to their customers of home equity-based loans for the purpose of building that share portfolio.

A $100 000 share portfolio with no deposit! Let your home help you build a fortune! And all for only $4800 cost per annum! Enticing?

Geared equities investment, however, potentially represents an even higher risk than negatively geared investment property. What the glossy print on the brochure doesn't tell you (it's only in the small print) is that the comparatively low costs are achieved *after* dividends are received. Generally, however, as explained below, you have to pay interest monthly and therefore the cash outlay is *much* higher than the $4800 mentioned. And tax deductions are not available until the *following* year. Look at the sums to see the traps.

For a special purpose home equity loan of $100 000 (interest rate, usually around 13 per cent and fixed for three years):

Interest on $100 000	$13 000
Dividends received (estimate)	$5 000
Net *loss*	$8 000
Tax deduction at tax rate, 43%	$3 440
Net *cost*	$4 560

Then, of course, the hope is that capital growth of, say, 10 per cent gives the underlying portfolio of $100 000 a $10 000 or more increase in value in the first year and so on. This compounding effect can provide untold riches in the future.

In three years, at this rate, the original $100 000 is worth $133 000. An increase in value of $33 000 and, after allowing for the *cost* of $4560 or $13 680 over the three years, it still provides you with a net gain of $19 320. And all this on no capital outlay!

Unfortunately, you don't get to keep your portfolio as the loan is a fixed interest-only loan (no capital reduction) so, at the end, has to be repaid or renegotiated. However, there are some other *realities* about the scheme.

First, the actual cash cost to you is much greater than the

$4560. Whereas interest is payable immediately (usually monthly), dividends occur only twice a year. And the tax deduction does not take effect until *at least* the following financial year. Thus, the cash outlay may be up to $12 000 or more.

Second, there is no guarantee — as is also the case in property investments — that the underlying value of the securities will rise. Indeed, over the short to medium term, say, one to three years, the values are liable to fluctuate very widely, and the real benefits of a share portfolio are generally not available for many years.

Third, job security is also a decisive factor. In the event of a job loss you may find yourself in a financial straight jacket.

These schemes are suitable for investors in the highest marginal tax bracket, and who can tolerate adverse circumstances both in terms of salary and share market falls. Otherwise, the only real beneficiaries are, once again, the banks.

Remember:

- Don't put up your home for negatively geared investment schemes without looking at all the risks.
- Negative gear only if you have genuine high marginal tax income and can afford to ride out any shocks.

Staying out of trouble

There are 10 easy steps to debt management:

1 Keep a budget.
2 Keep debts as low as possible.
3 Look at the costs involved.
4 Look for alternatives to credit.
5 Pay off credit card purchases every month — in full.
6 Borrow for investment not consumption.
7 Pay it off as quickly as possible.

8 Look at consolidating your debts.
9 Use debit cards; they allow you to use plastic to pay for purchases, but the money is taken out of your savings account so you don't actually borrow anything.
10 Be careful with credit cards and top-up schemes.

'Lines of credit can be a problem,' says Ms Hunter of Credit Help Line. 'People borrow up to $5000 and when it gets down to $4000 the company says you can top up to $5000 again the person is forever in debt and topping up. A lot of people fall behind in their repayments and have the repossessors or debt collectors at their door.'

What to do if you get into trouble

Talk to your creditors. Be honest — tell them you still intend to pay, that you've had a bit of a rough patch. Keep those lines of communication open. The worst thing you can do, if you are having financial problems, is to ignore them. Often creditors are willing to negotiate a mutually acceptable scheme to pay off the debts. Note also that most banks and lenders will waive interest payments under such a scheme. Some will even accept a settlement offer. It's the only advantage of getting into trouble!

Propose some form of interim payment. It shows good faith on your part. From your creditors' point of view, a part payment is better than nothing.

Get help. Counselling is recommended for people with financial problems — especially if they are related to other problems such as gambling, alcohol abuse or compulsive spending. Although counselling is not a panacea to irresponsibility.

Avoid bankruptcy. It's often possible for people facing bankruptcy to come to an unofficial arrangement with their creditors.

Consolidate your debts. It's worthwhile amalgamating your debt if you can do it. First write it all down and then talk to your bank manager about it.

If you can't consolidate your debts, pay off those with high interest rates first.

When taking out a loan you should consider whether you would be able to meet repayments if your income were reduced through disability, sickness or injury. Shop around for an insurance deal if this worries you. Ask for three types of quotes:

1. *Life cover.* Designed to provide payment of the outstanding balance of your loan account in the event of your death.
2. *Life and critical illness cover.* Designed to provide payment of the outstanding balance of your loan account in the event of your death or upon diagnosis of any of a number of critical illnesses.
3. *Disablement cover.* Designed to meet your loan repayments in the event of you being unable to work due to injury or sickness.

Remember that workers' compensation or sickness benefits do not usually match your previous income, and life cover under superannuation may not be enough to meet your debts.

Alternatives to bank finance

In general only one or two alternatives offer distinct advantages over a bank loan; for example, insurance policy loans. If your insurance policy has a specified cash surrender value — that is, a cash reserve that is available to you on termination of your policy — the insurance company may be a source of a low-interest loan. Check it out.

There are two other alternatives:

- *Credit unions* are one of the main providers of personal finance. They are particularly strong in the area of motor vehicle finance.
- *Debit cards* allow you to use plastic to pay for purchases but the money is taken out of your savings account so you don't need to borrow money.

Save for it

Helen saved $25 a week for three years, meanwhile earning 6 per cent on her money. She purchased a second-hand car for $4000, plus insurance.

Frank buys the same car but borrows the money. His repayments are $32 per week, paying just over 13 per cent interest.

Frank is paying a higher monthly rate than Helen, but he does have the car three years before she does.

Choose which situation you prefer.

Six steps to loan management

- Consumables such as clothes, cars and holidays are good to have but they do diminish in value. Try to avoid borrowing for these. Assets like a home, business or shares are more viable to borrow for.
- Negotiate on entry fees with your bank if you are in the market for a personal loan. Many banks are getting rid of such fees. It is a good negotiating point as the banks don't have a lot of leeway on interest rates.

- Be wary of *flat rate* interest deals. They are usually only offered by finance companies and are not reducible. Interest is continuously charged on the original principal, thus making these a very expensive form of finance.
- Shop around. Look for features such as flexible repayment plans with no early repayment penalties.
- Attempt to have all your loans at the one institution. This is helpful for consolidation plans.
- Always consider alternatives to borrowing; for example, save, before going into debt. Debt is a serious step, particularly for young people.

Chapter 8

Beating the banks

Elaine Wilkinson was a fastidious woman who kept the family's accounts. Being fiercely independent she knew exactly where every dollar was spent. Elaine realised at a very early stage that a carefree approach to finances was a careless one.

'I wanted a debt-free existence. I didn't want to keep having a 25-year mortgage in front of me.

'When I got pregnant with our second child two years ago, I knew that money would be tight when I stopped working. We were a two-income family and we had borrowed to our limits when we bought the house.

'I looked at all our spending patterns, including shopping, and saw that we were throwing away $400 a month in bad money habits, including bank fees and interest, and poor spending.

'I knew if I re-organised things I would be able make a real dent on our spending. It made a difference and we were able to manage until I went back to work. I consolidated all our bank accounts into one and linked a savings account to the mortgage — an offset account. We ended up paying virtually no bank fees.

'I also found out that it would save us tax if the interest earned on our savings account got credited to our mortgage rather than added to our savings. The extra money left over each month — it wasn't much — usually \$80–\$100, much of what we pulled back from the bank in fees and interest charges — went straight into the offset account.

'It wasn't until recently that I realised something very exciting was happening. I looked at our bank statement for the mortgage account and asked the bank how much longer before it would be paid out at the current rate of repayments — \$1090 rather than \$990 per month.

'To my surprise, we would have our mortgage paid out in five years. We had chopped seven years off the mortgage! It was like finding a pot of gold.'

You can save \$60 000 in bank interest on your mortgage. The savings you'll make by running fee-free banking can be converted to your own *pot of gold*. The steps to achieve this are simple enough, but there are pitfalls. This chapter will examine the various ways of reaching this goal.

The Wilkinsons had saved seven years of bank interest — a total of \$61 000. That is, \$61 000 in their pockets and not in the bank's coffers. All of it came from clawing back a mere \$100 per month from the bank. In doing so they had given themselves a real chance of achieving financial independence at an age when most are still lumbering under the twin burdens of debt and a large amount of monthly income tied up.

For many, *mortgage* is a word loaded with unpleasant emotions, often creating high anxiety in an already stress-filled existence. Most of us accept interest costs associated with our mortgages as a necessary evil. Most of us are grateful for the opportunity to build an asset to enjoy in the later stages of our lives. Few of us wonder how to beat the system. Remember, it was only a few years ago that mortgage money was effectively tied up by the banks, giving them enormous power over us. This power was often exercised in the form of excessively high interest rates, high (and often hidden) costs, and little flexibility once we committed to the mortgage.

The dollars involved for home borrowers are just too big to ignore and to leave unattended. A typical mortgage of $100 000 at 8.9 per cent over 25 years is costing you around $832 per month. That's $249 708 over the full 25 years of the loan — or $149 708 in interest payments alone. But, as you saw in the Wilkinsons' case, you can beat the blow-out — deprive the banks of tens of thousands of dollars — and profit from it. The solution is simple. Just pump every extra cent you have into the loan — even if it's only a few dollars a week. That's a simple step that the average person or family can do straight away. (Again, as we noted in Chapter 7, be aware some fixed interest accounts incur penalties for early repayment.)

Simple steps to beat the banks

Doing it quicker will save you money. By paying the mortgage off in 20 or even 15 years you'll save tens of thousands of dollars. This is money you will have that your bank won't have.

Make your repayments more often. Paying your loan off fortnightly will make a big difference to your loan. This is because there are 26 fortnights in a year while there are only 12 months (26 fortnights are 13 lots of four weeks). It may sound too good to be true, but it really does work.

Hit the principal. Put that tax refund or any other lump sum to good work. You can even put your salary to work. While it may seem like a waste or an opportunity foregone to dump all that extra money into the mortgage, it will save you thousands in the long run. You will be making a sound investment by paying off your own home sooner. There is no better investment. Consider this. Once your home is paid off, it will be appreciating at an average of 5 per cent per annum. On a $200 000 home, this means you are gaining $10 000 tax-free dollars per year!

Getting your money back: redraw. As we saw in Chapter 6 most lenders these days offer redraw facilities. In effect this type of facility allows you to *take back* any money you have paid over and above the standard repayments. This allows you to put money towards the mortgage that you have no immediate need for, meanwhile decreasing the principal and saving interest, but being secure in the knowledge that you can get it if you need it.

Run an offset account. Offset accounts run in a similar fashion to the redraw facilities. The difference is that the money in the offset account is yours and you can access it at any time for any purpose. Offset accounts are very tax effective with the interest earned offset against your mortgage and therefore not taxable in your hands.

So, with an offset account any interest you earn is used to reduce — or offset — the interest charged on your mortgage. Why it saves you so much is because it substantially reduces the compounding effect of interest that you are paying on your mortgage. Put everything you've got into your loan!

Assume you have savings of $5000 sitting in a savings account earning interest. You receive interest on that deposit which must then be declared as assessable income in your tax return. You could end up paying up to half back to the tax man. Meanwhile, you are still applying interest on the full amount outstanding on your mortgage.

What if you had $5000 in an offset account earning 5 per cent interest — $250 a year. The bank credits this to your mortgage account. This amount is equivalent to around $20 per month. On an average mortgage this $20 a month alone can save over $20 000 in interest over the full term of the loan, reducing the term by more than two years!

While researching this book I asked one of my friends — a merchant banker type who is savvy and meticulous — how he organised his mortgage, hoping to find another *hero*. I was not disappointed.

'I never see my salary cheque. It gets paid directly into my MLC mortgage account — their Home First product. They immediately credit the amount against the outstanding mortgage. The principal is reduced immediately every time my salary electronically hits the account.

'I set up my ANZ access account as a nominated account and I simply sweep funds across every time I need funds. I have ATM access and cheque book access to my money whenever I need it.

'I know MLC's rate is a fraction higher than some of the cheapest, and I do recall paying an up-front fee. But there are no ongoing fees. What it does is force me to budget. You see, I get one free ad hoc withdrawal a month; you really need to work out exactly what bills have to be regularly paid and how much you need to live on so that you can leave any spare money paying off your mortgage.

'You have to take out the amount your budget says you are going to spend, so your savings are already in the mortgage making it that much harder to get your hands on it.

'But you tell me where I can get a better return for my money — all my money?'

I sat down with Phil and calculated the effect of this arrangement: he was three years into his $150 000 mortgage and he was well on the way to paying it off in under half the original 25 years. And no bank fees!

He drew $300 a week for groceries and other living expenses, and $1000 a month for other bills. He worked out he was putting an extra $400 a month into his mortgage account — and not doing without. At this rate Phil would have his home paid off completely in 10 years, saving him over $87 000 in interest.

What is available today for consumers is nothing short of revolutionary. With no extra money — that is, your current salary alone — you can save tens of thousands of dollars by opening up or converting to this type of loan: a savings and loan account rolled into one. There is simply no inconvenience to the scheme and virtually no extra fees. The cost of the 0.25 per cent premium in the variable rates charged are small when compared to the benefits.

Start now

Although the best results will come if you follow the principles of minimising bank fees and charges outlined earlier in this book, and put into practice by the Wilkinsons, a good starting point can be in ensuring that your home loan offers you a *mortgage offset account* facility. Apart from an offset account, most lending institutions will today also offer redraw facilities on all but the most basic home loans. The disadvantage of redraw facilities is that fees often apply to each redraw, with some institutions requiring minimum redraws of $5000. Check the minimum balance required by your bank for an offset savings deposit. Check their rates and try and negotiate for *full* offset.

Banks today offer an added flexibility, such as that which was taken up by the Wilkinsons. In a transactions-based account, where money flow is more flexible, withdrawals and deposits are made according to the needs of the account holder. This puts some of the control back in your hands. The savings style offset account, meanwhile, is designed for customers not needing to access funds too regularly, thus attracting a higher rate of interest.

As we saw earlier, fees are a consideration for high volume transactions accounts, and can be a trap for unwary customers. They vary widely between institutions and you will need to establish the number of transactions you can make before additional fees cut in.

As far as the lower interest rate offered on such accounts is concerned, consider this: extra money paid into a home loan with a rate of, say, 9.5 per cent, saves you the full 9.5 per cent. Money paid instead into an offset account will usually save you a few percentage points less, around 6 per cent.

Tip: Ask your bank which interest rate applies: rates can vary greatly. Negotiate with your bank to offer you term deposit rates!

Number crunching: increasing your monthly repayments

Consider a typical $100 000 mortgage currently on a variable 8.8 per cent rate for 25 years. Current repayments are $826 per month. However, look at the monthly repayments required to repay the same mortgage in:

20 years	$887
15 years	$1002

The difference between:

- 25 years and 20 years is an extra payment of $60 per month but in fact this saves you $34 920 in interest.

- 25 years and 15 years is an extra payment of $176 per month but in fact this saves you $67 440 in interest.

Cutting the term will save interest — how this works is calculated below.

Term: 25 years; interest rate: 8.8%;	
Monthly payment	$826
Total payments	$826 × 300
	= $247 800
Total interest paid	$247 800 – $100 000
	= $147 800
Term: 20 years	
Monthly payments	$887.00
Total payments	$887 × 240
	= $212 880
Total interest paid	$212 880 – $100 000
	=$112 880
Term: 15 years	
Monthly payments	$1002
Total payments	$1002 × 180
	= $180 360
Total interest paid	$180 360 – $100 000
	= $80 360

Interest saved by paying an extra $60 a month to reduce the term from 25 years to 20 years, for example, is $34 920 ($147 800 – $112 880). So by paying an extra $60 a month for 240 months (20 years), that is $14 400, you *save* $34 920!

In all cases, interest rates remained the same. And while a

steady interest rate is not a realistic expectation, interest rates will rise *and* fall over the term of the loan.

These savings are extraordinary and have been checked by a firm of chartered accountants. They are free from income and capital gains tax, and have been structured in such a way as to shelter your gains from the tax collector.

Congratulations you are now a canny investor

Just to put the gains into perspective, consider what you would need to earn on an alternative investment to generate, for example, $34 900 after tax over 20 years.

If your marginal tax rate is, say, 34 per cent you would need to generate $52 900 gross income over 20 years — that's more than $2600 each year to match these returns. You have paid an extra $60 per month over 20 years — an amount of $14 400. The return on your money you would need to achieve would be more than 20 per cent per annum!

Paying extra off your mortgage is a great investment. It is simply not possible to find other investments that can achieve these rates of return with the same degree of safety and tax effectiveness.

More importantly for those with other debts — such as a car loan, personal loan or a credit card debt — the real question is: should I pay off my mortgage with my disposable income, or should I pay off my other debts sooner?

Let's look at the following example. If the interest rate charged on a loan was 20 per cent (and that's the level for a number of credit card providers, for example), and this interest was not tax deductable, you would need a 30 per cent annual return from a fully taxed income-only investment to match the 20 per cent annual interest charge (assuming a marginal tax rate of 34 cents in the dollar).

It is obvious that completely unattainable investment returns would be required on a pre-tax basis to match the after-tax rate of the interest you are paying on your loan. It is therefore worthwhile to pay off these high interest debts sooner. You will need to check that there are no penalties associated with early repayment. Certainly, credit card debts do not incur such penalties.

What happens when interest rates change?

For those on variable rate loans, changes in interest rates can be dealt with in several ways. When banks raise their rates, for example, many banks offer borrowers the option of paying extra per month and thus maintaining the original term of the loan. Or alternatively, borrowers can maintain their rate of repayments but increase the term of their loan. However, most banks will put a cap of 25 years on this.

But for the purposes of the exercise — that is, to save interest and pay off your home early — it is important not to go backwards. It is necessary therefore to opt for the higher monthly repayment. On the other hand, when interest rates fall, maintain the current rate of repayment to achieve the desired outcome of an earlier repayment of the mortgage.

Putting it all together

Arnold saw the power of early home ownership. He put his savings into a mortgage account and put every spare cent into his mortgage. He didn't have to pay income tax on the interest which he would have paid on the savings.

He used his increased home equity to finance a small investment property. Because he was a PAYE taxpayer, he calculated that, since he was going to be claiming a tax deduction on the investment property (being the difference between the net rental income and the interest paid), he would be entitled to a reduced monthly PAYE tax deduction, which meant that he would have more cash in his pocket each fortnight.

Excited by his new-found financial freedom, Arnold kept looking for avenues whereby he could further beat the system. He had already reduced his costs of doing business with the banks by 90 per cent, saving him more than $2000 in bank fees and charges, FID and other government taxes per annum, as well as maximising the return on his savings account.

Because he was a professional and able to claim a proportion of the use of his car for income-related usage, Arnold calculated that he could improve his financial position even further if he leased his new motor vehicle. He maximised this by taking the $7000 trade-in he received from his old car and paying it straight into his mortgage.

By doing that Arnold knocked seven years off it, saving $30 000 in interest payments. The $400 per month lease payments for four years (partially tax deductable) were small compared with the savings generated).

Arnold figured that you didn't have to be a genius to work out that by doing this you saved the 9.5 per cent mortgage rate after tax, and although the lease costs — which were partially tax deductable — were high at 11.5 per cent, it was a no contest — even when depreciation costs were taken into account.

It should not come as a surprise to find Arnold now in semi-retirement, cruising his yacht in Queensland's magnificent Whitsunday Passage, and living comfortably off the income from several investment properties.

Renovate without debt

What would you rather do: move house, renovate, or eat a live scorpion? None of these are attractive propositions for most of us. But there does come a time to consider the first two propositions at least. And as living rooms around the country abound with horror stories — like the Lewis's in the previous chapter — many families are electing not to move but rather renovate.

We are experiencing a boom in renovation, and it seems to make a lot of financial sense. Because we all know that apart from the financial risks of moving, the costs in terms of stamp duty and other charges can add another $15 000 to the new home purchase.

A well-designed renovation will almost always improve accommodation, and unless the renovation is over the top, the cost will, over time, pay dividends in terms of a much higher valuation on your property. So, despite the impact on our nerves and health, renovating starts to look attractive, particularly if you plan your finances correctly. And there is no reason to pay penalty rates of interest to carry it through — the days of the painful second mortgage are long gone!

Get your bank to pay your renovation at no additional cost

Sounds like a slick ad campaign doesn't it? We all know that renovations sap not only our finances but also our patience, often exceeding budgets and leaving bank accounts depleted, despite new and existing loans. Yet, as far as paying off the home earlier and the examples outlined above, nothing has changed. Rather than be discouraged to commence such plans, you should note that any start to reducing the term of the mortgage — before or after the renovations — is a good start.

With the recent proliferation of flexible mortgages, offering, for example, redraw facilities, ploughing all savings direct into a mortgage makes perfect sense. Moreover, your higher equity gained through additional payments will place you in an excellent position to borrow money for that extension or renovation.

What is available, if you have been making those extra repayments on your loan, is the ability to redraw the amount, which may be enough to cover the cost of the work.

A five-step action plan

1 Check whether your current lender will offer you a transaction style facility on your mortgage account which allows your salary to be paid electronically directly into your mortgage. Withdraw small amounts weekly rather than larger amounts monthly for living expenses. That way your money is saving you mortgage interest for that extra week or two every month.

2 Open an offset account for your savings. Avoid paying tax on any interest earned by running the account. Look at a transaction style offset account if you need regular accessing of the funds. Rates may be lower for the increased flexibility. And watch the fees!

3 Repay your mortgage every fortnight. Most banks today will allow you the option of repaying your loan fortnightly instead of monthly. Consider this seriously because if your mortgage — like most — is calculated on daily balance, you'll save thousands in the process. It makes sense particularly as many families receive fortnightly salary or wage cheques. It is therefore easier to budget on a fortnightly basis *and* particularly easy if you have your transaction account linked to your mortgage.

4 Ask your bank to work out how much extra you would need to pay to reduce the term of your mortgage by: (a) 5 years and (b) 10 years.

5 Put lump sums to work. Put them into your mortgage and make sure you can redraw in the future should you need to.

Chapter 9

Credit cards

While eating his Weeties, John thrust a newspaper in front of Mary. 'Look at this, Qantas and Telstra have just brought out this new card. I'm going to apply for one.'

'But you already have a Telstra Visa card.'

'This one gives us points towards free air travel.'

'But you're already a member of Golden Wings and you get lots of bonus points there don't you?'

'Mary, you don't understand. This is not just about bonus points. Look, the Telstra Visa card not only gives us the chance to get free clothes or a new stereo, but also points towards free air travel every time we use it to pay a bill. You need to keep up with the latest.'

John's breakfast remained untouched. Mary knew the signs — it was useless to argue. John was hooked.

John was a junkie. Not your ordinary powder-snorting or pill-popping variety — John was hooked on plastic. Credit cards and charge cards. John couldn't get enough of them. At last count he had 40! And just as junkies can injure their health, John's habit had injured both his and his family's financial health.

Despite a very good income as an IT consultant to the Australian subsidiary of a large US corporation, John always seemed to struggle to make ends meet. Yes, John and Mary had accumulated thousands of credit points towards air travel, new appliances, vacations and a new car. But they were strapped for cash.

John had been seduced by the marketing whiz kids who have created new product areas for organisations such as Telstra and Qantas to move into. These new *loyalty* programs, as they are called, and co-branded schemes have transformed the Australian credit card market.

Banks have now joined forces with companies such as General Motors and Telstra and have drawn in many new cardholders by offering incentives ranging from discounts on cars to waiving the first year's card fee. And while new card offers appear daily in our letter box or in the media, existing operators are finding more ways to keep us on the hook. If you believe what you read, Australians now count their points when they shop.

Fortunately, most of us have more mundane problems when it comes to credit cards. We're tempted to buy that new CD or to go to that special restaurant before having to juggle the bills knowing that not paying the credit card in time will cost dearly in interest charges. Ever since the bankcard assault of the 1970s Australians have had a love/hate relationship with the credit card.

There are clever new card marketing schemes being thrust at us daily and banks continue to charge very high interest rates on credit cards. We need to be ever vigilant in our use of credit cards. The following sections will guide you through some of the basics — the types of cards available, choosing the best credit card, and running it without paying the banks any interest.

Loyalty cards: the con

Since ANZ launched it's Telstra Visa card in 1995 it has gained more than 500 000 new cardholders, tapped largely from Telstra's giant customer base. The complementary Qantas Telstra Visa card was launched to appeal to people who want travel-focused rewards. This too has been a runaway success, according to the marketing whiz kids. The scheme now boasts more than 100 000 members.

Who can argue? Everyone loves a freebie. If two products are much of a muchness, the one with the freebies looks tempting. *But are these loyalty cards of any real benefit?*

Some calculations show that there are some 40 or so features that can be attached to credit cards including access to a 24-hour help desk (to find more ways of spending money?), automatic periodic payments, an emergency message service, travel and life insurance, wine clubs, hotel discounts, and free tax and legal advice. This is a big change from 10 years ago when most credit cards came with 55 interest-free days and little else.

Banks, card issuers such as Visa and Master Card, and companies like Telstra, Coles Myer, Qantas and General Motors-Holden have all formed alliances based on loyalty schemes. What you will earn in benefits, if anything, depends on your spending power, shopping habits and whether the reward is attainable within the permitted time frame. At best, it may represent a small discount, from as low as 3 per cent, and at worst you may never qualify for anything. As always, big spenders, especially business travellers, benefit most.

Every time you use your charge or credit card, you are awarded points based on the dollar value of the purchase. But you can speed things up by earning bonus points using the scheme's participating partners, which could be petrol stations, supermarkets, hotels, airlines, car rental, and so on.

Ultimately you have to ask yourself whether it's worth driving miles out of your way to buy something of which you are not entirely sure. 'As a golden rule consumers shouldn't change their spending habits just to receive a few incentives, but if you can get something for nothing, why not?' advises Chris Gosselin, managing director of Market Faxts, the interest rate monitoring group.

He suggests that consumers should look at the types of cards available and match them to their lifestyle in order to extract maximum benefits. 'If you're a busy executive who travels on business regularly, flies often and eats out for business, then maybe. But if you're an everyday type of spender and want to accumulate points gradually, *Fly Buys* may be a better option.'

Fly Buys have been running since August 1994. The *Fly Buys* card put out by National Australia Bank, Coles Myer and Shell has attracted two million customers since its inception. Here, for example, a member would need to spend about $188 a week over a year to accumulate 850 points; that is, a total spending of about $10 000. The 850 points would earn the equivalent of a return ticket between Sydney and Melbourne. To put this into perspective, according to the Australian Bureau of Statistics, weekly expenditure of $250 on groceries, petrol and other shopping items is typical for the average family.

Comparing *reward* programs between cards is not easy but the bottom lines are: Is the interest rate competitive, does it have interest-free days? What's the point of incurring a large interest bill when the cost of the interest could provide the reward? Remember, that the whole purpose of these cards is to enhance *loyalty* to both the bank and its co-brander.

NSW Graduate School of Management associate professor of marketing Grahame Dowling believes loyalty programs are overrated which invariably cost businesses money and antagonise customers.

Peter Kell, of the Australian Consumers' Association, says consumers should not be sucked in by the marketing hype. 'In most cases the benefits are likely to be fairly ordinary. You could probably achieve them yourself by shopping around. First and foremost you should make sure you get a good deal in terms of interest rates and fees and charges on your card before you get sucked into the glossy add-ons.'

For many consumers, even an impressive number of points may ultimately amount to nothing in terms of material benefits. The banks have managed to cleverly pitch *value-added* products at us in order to justify exorbitantly high interest rates.

The benefit of loyalty cards may be debatable but what is certain is that, at a more mundane level, credit cards are expensive. All of us have suffered credit card *indigestion* at some time. Jane's story is typical of many I have heard.

Jane has little money left after paying her rent and living expenses. Like many of us she wants the small luxuries of life. Jane can't resist a new outfit, nor can she resist the lure of some warm, tropical island during a cold, wintry Melbourne night. A booking on her Visa card is a breeze.

Jane always charges her night out with friends on her Amex card. And her store account card allows her to pay for gifts and life's little luxuries.

Although Jane makes a monthly payment towards her Visa and Amex cards, she can't ever seem to clear them. Her last statements showed a $2900 balance on her Visa account and a $850 balance on Amex, while her David Jones account had a debit balance of $400.

'I'm quite comfortable with what I owe at the moment. I try and keep under a few thousand. I don't know exactly what it costs me or what the interest rate is but it is lifestyle.'

While not extraordinary, Jane's case will help illustrate the real cost of reckless use of credit cards.

Many customers do not know what rate they pay and most would not know that interest rates range from 12.5 to 21.95 per cent (the higher figure being for some store cards). It *is* costly and lifestyle benefits aside, the only real beneficiaries are the banks and the retailers. While John's credit card habit is beyond calculation, Jane's is just plain expensive.

At current rates of interest (around 16 per cent on credit cards), Jane is paying around $700 a year in interest charges — about $58 every month. Not a huge amount of money, but enough to keep her from getting full control of her finances.

The credit card habit

Where did this all start and how does it affect us? Some may recall the launch of the bankcard back in the 1970s. With great fanfare and an avalanche of unsolicited free credit cards we were sucked into the brave, wondrous world of plastic credit by the banks. The cards went to all and sundry.

At the time I was a business proprietor and my Bankcard limit was set at $2000. An employee of mine, a 21-year-old man arrived at work one morning very pleased with himself, announcing that he'd been granted a credit ceiling of $5000. It seemed like such an assault — testing a young person's ability to resist temptation.

Credit cards were introduced to make money for the banks — and not just to make it easier for you to buy things when you don't have money to pay for them on the spot. At last count — and these are unofficial figures — there were over 200 different types of credit cards available.

Australia is among the most credit hungry countries on earth. According to Reserve Bank statistics, each year we swallow $25 billion of new credit — much of it through credit cards. Latest Reserve Bank figures showed that credit card usage is booming. There are almost 7 million credit card accounts in Australia, on which more than $7 billion is outstanding, up 20 per cent over the year. Seven billion dollars owed to the banks! That's an average of over $1000 per account — meaning at least $2000 per family.

So strong is the lure of plastic to banks and their customers that in the United States, for example (which, after all, is a glimpse of the future as far as we in Australia are concerned), supermarkets and milk bars routinely accept credit payment as a substitute for cash or cheques. Households are bombarded with offers from credit card banks, often linked to attractions such as frequent-flier points. America's casino boom has allowed gamblers to use their credit cards to borrow cash on the spot to bet on games of chance.

Credit card banks in the US now compete furiously for the first business of university students. Even though these young borrowers have little current income, they tend to remain loyal to their first card.

Credit cards: how to avoid interest

Banks make money on both sides of the credit card transaction. There are interest payments and annual fees on one side, and merchant fees on the other. Each time you use the card the merchant pays up to 5 per cent for accepting the card. So it's not hard to see why banks encourage the proliferation of credit cards.

The rates you pay on your card are at a premium because of the bank's strangle hold on the supply of credit. But you don't have to pay a cent if you manage your card carefully.

Although interest rates have fallen they are yet to be

reflected in the rates charged on cards, which range between 12.5 and 19.0 per cent, giving the banks huge profit margins. Remarkably, these margins have been cut back from the much higher margins which prevailed a few years ago when it took government intervention to force the banks to lower their profit margins. At that time, some banks were charging credit card holders up to 30 per cent interest!

Even now, banks often refuse to lower credit card rates, even though deposit rates have already fallen. Pegged at about 5 percentage points above the mortgage rates for most of the past three years, card rates now stand on average a massive 6 per cent above mortgage rates!

According to Chris Gosselin of Market Faxts there's a good reason banks won't cut credit card rates. 'That's to maximise their profit margins. There's been so much focus on the home loan market that they think that no-one will notice if they don't move credit card rates.'

A cut in official interest rates, by way of illustration, reduces the cost to banks of providing credit, therefore any delay in passing on the cut to home and credit card borrowers boosts their profit margin. 'But,' suggests Chris Gosselin, 'the banks do need to charge a higher rate on credit cards. First it is unsecured credit and for that the consumer must pay. If a borrower defaults on the loan the bank has nothing to fall back on.

'Second, it is revolving credit so there is an advantage to the consumer in being able to run it up and down. Third, there is a very high transactional cost: the card holder could make many $10 purchases in a month, causing a lot of paper work for the banks. And fourth, many consumers use the free period very effectively so the banks need to be able to recover interest from the rest of the customers that have debit balances.'

We all end up paying dearly because banks can't make money by applying *normal* interest rates to credit cards. So how is it that cuts in official interest rates can pass fairly quickly from the banks to consumers in the home lending market and not elsewhere such as in credit card market? The answer lies in competition.

According to Chris Gosselin the banks have lost so much margin in their home lending products that they need to recover it elsewhere. 'Credit cards are one place they can recover this lost margin because it is not interest rate sensitive like the home loan market. However, with the entry of some non-banks into the market we might see some price competition.'

Gosselin does caution that even when banks do drop rates there is often a *bite* elsewhere. Take, for example, the rate cut late last year by the Commonwealth Bank. While dropping the interest rate on its 55-day interest-free cards by 0.25 percentage points to 16.7 per cent, the Commonwealth Bank joined in cancelling the interest-free period on new purchases if the previous month's account had not been paid in full.

In effect, the change increased the amount of interest paid by customers who use the 55-day interest-free cards as a revolving line of credit, rather than as a debt repaid in full within the month. This change can nearly double the interest paid by Commonwealth Bank customers who do not pay their total bill by the due date.

Peter Kell of the Australian Consumers' Association (ACA) criticised the way some banks' interest charges were explained to customers, where descriptions of the changes gave 'no clear indication' that the changes would cost some customers more.

'It's another classic example of putting out something that's hard to understand and can have a major impact on credit card users. Consumers aren't getting the sort of deals they deserve. The banks are too comfortable in this market. There is little or no genuine competition on credit rates between banks.'

Even the Banking Ombudsman in his 1995 annual report

has said: 'Given (these) complicated charging arrangements, many customers are confused by the explanations contained in the conditions of use provided by card issuers.'

Poor credit card use

It is a sad fact of life that people get into trouble by buying on credit when they can ill afford to. But there are some basics in good credit card *habits*, and we will outline these in the following pages. Unfortunately, no one can advise you what your priorities should be. If you get overwhelmed by your debt it's important to take stock. If you believe that a credit card is controlling you rather than the other way around, then it's time to cut it up.

What's your plastic profile?

Do you intend to:

— pay back on time and rarely get cash advances?

— sometimes use credit or obtain cash advances or forget to pay on time?

What are your usual number of transactions per month?

Andrew Woods, general manager of the credit section of the Credit Reference Association of Australia, Australia's principal credit referral service, says: 'Although most of the population behave in a financially responsible way there are people who can't manage their finances, and credit cards get them into more trouble. We have many credit card defaulters on our books and more often than not these people should never have been given credit.'

The cycle is frightening in its simplicity. The borrower fills the card, pays the minimum, then goes to the bank for an increase on the limit. 'Generally the lower your income the more likely you are to subsidise your income with credit,' says Deborah Hunter, a counsellor at the Sydney-based Credit

Helpline. 'If you are using it to subsidise your income it's a potential path for disaster.'

In fact, figures published by the federal Attorney-General last September show that personal bankruptcies were increasing and that one of the most common causes of personal bankruptcy was people abusing credit cards and continually committing themselves to debt.

Good and bad credit habits start from a young age. A recent government secondary school report found that most teenagers surveyed had debit cards. In theory these are not credit cards as they operate from an amount already in the account. However, in spite of assurances to the contrary by the banks it is possible to overdraw money in a debit account.

This early involvement with debit cards inevitably means a progression into the use of credit cards. It is a multi-million dollar business for banks to get young people well and truly involved, first in the use of debit cards and subsequently with credit cards.

Because the banks do not check with each other about their customers it is possible for people (indeed a large proportion do) to have several credit cards. This is a sure-fire path to over-commitment. You should limit yourself to only one credit card — at the most!

Plastic fantastic: charge or credit card?

Credit cards have an ongoing line of credit with outstanding balances charged interest while charge cards have set fee structures but outstandings must be paid off monthly.

American Express and Diners Club are charge cards. That means they provide credit for a limited period — from the date of purchase until the *date due* on the statement. You pay a joining fee and an annual membership fee. You are required to pay your account each month. These don't give automatic access to an extended line of credit, enabling you to avoid the risk of spending money you don't have. The main attraction of these cards is that they don't have a set limit on the amount that can be charged against the cards and are useful for Eftpos purchases at supermarkets.

Bankcard, Mastercard and many Visa cards are credit cards. That means they provide continuous or revolving lines of credit. You are required to pay off a minimum proportion each month but you can leave the rest owing and pay interest on it. Membership or joining fees are not usually charged.

The most used credit card is still Bankcard, which is issued by the big four banks and some state banks. The drawback here is that while this is almost universally accepted in Australia it can't be used overseas.

In contrast, two of the overseas credit cards, Visa and Mastercard, give a slightly more limited coverage within Australia, but have wide acceptance in the USA, much of Europe and in Asia. These cards are widely used for both purchases and ATM cash withdrawals.

These two types of cards offer two distinct services. The repay monthly balance card generally has an interest-free period, which encourages holders to repay in full as the interest rate after this term is steep, usually 15 to 16.5 per cent. In the past few years, since the split in credit card products was introduced, these accounts have attracted annual fees of between $20 and $30.

The more popular credit cards — accounting for about two-thirds of all card transactions — don't require the monthly balance to be repaid. Instead it is carried on each month, accruing interest at a rate slightly lower than the interest-free period card, generally 15 to 15.95 per cent. This type of card once avoided annual fees, but more banks have been introducing ongoing charges.

Beating the banks

Pay no interest! Most of these credit cards offer an interest-free period on purchases until 25 days after the date of statement, meaning, in effect, up to a 55-day free credit period. Any amount owing at the end of this period of grace incurs interest charges. Cash advances don't come with an interest-free period. Interest is charged on a daily basis from the date of the transaction.

If you pay off the amount within the interest-free period it doesn't matter what interest rate applies as no interest is charged. If you are not going to pay off the card monthly you should also know when the interest kicks in. It can be from the date of purchase, the statement date, and it can make a big difference to the amount of interest you pay.

Remember: If your credit card requires the full amount to be paid you must pay the whole amount to avoid credit charges. If you pay the whole amount less one dollar, then under the conditions of use the bank will charge interest on the whole amount.

Using credit cards often feels like getting something for nothing, at least until the bill arrives. Get into a routine of *good* account practice:

Let's say your bankcard balance is $1200; your required monthly payment is $60 and you made $100 new purchases this month. To get rid of this debt (if you don't have the full amount) pay $210 to cover the following:

New purchase amount	$100
Required monthly payment	$60
Additional principle payment	$50
Total payment	$210

You can pay off your credit card balance in half the time with manageable extra principle payments. You need to put in the extra principle repayment otherwise your credit card debt will never be paid off. The only winner will be the bank.

Questions to ask when looking for the right credit card

- Is there an interest-free period?
- What is the interest rate?
- When does the rate apply: from purchase date, statement or due date?
- Are there transaction charges?
- What is the bank's position if I can't pay my card off?
- Are there any charges if I pay each month?

Shopping for credit

'Shopping around for the right credit card is a nightmare,' says Peter Kell of the ACA. 'But you need to do it because the credit card-charging regime is outrageous. It's a complex product, and most people have a high degree of inertia when it comes to changing their card and their habits — they just don't have the time to shop around.'

If you believe the convenience of a credit card outweighs the danger of never being able to pay it off you need to be aware of what's what in credit cards. With so many cards around, not only is there a risk of abuse but it is easy to end up with a card that is inappropriate for your lifestyle and spending habits. Like home loans the question these days is do you really need a Rolls-Royce when the basic Holden will do the job?

Chris Gosselin says the first step in choosing a credit card should be to take an honest look at your spending patterns and how you use your card, rather than jumping in on the basis of interest rate costs alone. He identifies two types of credit card users — *borrowers* and *transactors*. Borrowers use cards to borrow money (either cash advances or purchases) against available credit limits. Transactors, on the other hand, use credit cards exclusively for purchasing goods and services. Gosselin recommends borrowers look for the lowest interest rate while transactors should make the most of interest-free days and extra benefits.

The borrower is also the one who is most likely to head for financial disaster, paying the minimum then going back to the bank for an increase to the limit.

Chris Gosselin believes the interest rate is not the way to identify the right card. 'You can use one that charges 15 or 16 per cent and a $26 annual fee, but doesn't give you any interest-free days if you don't pay it off. That could blow out your budgets. 'And shopping around is very important because on credit cards such as Visa and Bankcard rates can range from 12.5 to 16.75 per cent. Store-based cards are even higher, going up to 22 per cent in some cases.

'However interest-free days are beneficial to people using their credit card in certain ways. For example, some cards charge high interest rates, yet can be cheap if used properly. If there are no annual fees, you have 25 interest-free days, and the correct way is to pay in full, and if you pay in full it's a very cheap card. If you use it as revolving credit and don't pay it off, it's a very expensive card.'

Unfortunately, most of us fall into the trap of using credit cards very extensively over the festive season, first to buy gifts, then to charge up all kinds of holiday-related spending: air fares, accommodation, restaurants, and so on. Very few are able to clear these indulgences without first incurring several months of punishingly high interest costs.

Accordingly, the best card would be one that still offers an interest-free period, despite not having a nil balance carried froward and a low interest rate. Both St George Visa card and Commonwealth Bank Gold Visa offer interest-free days and a relatively low interest rate. Both also calculate interest on purchases from the statement date not the purchase date, giving a slight advantage on new purchases.

Credit card Blow-out: what to do

This is a phenomenon we have all encountered! But a serious one for those that simply can't escape the spiral.

Jim, aged 23, is a carpenter who had a very enjoyable Xmas. He took a holiday to Byron Bay for a few weeks and relaxed by the beach. Meanwhile, he ran up credit card debts exceeding $2300. By February the interest bill was exceeding his minimum payments. But Jim hated being in debt, so he fronted up to the bank — the credit card provider — and offered them a cash settlement of $2000. They accepted.

The truth: some cards are a status symbol

When I was offered one of those gold cards by Amex, I felt quite chuffed — wealthy, in fact. A $10 000 card limit! Just think about it, $10 000 available — instantly. But, despite this feeling of new-found wealth I never spent over $2000 in any month and (nearly) always paid off the card each time. So why did I need to pay extra fees for a gold card? Prestige. And prestige always costs.

In the case of *gold* cards, invariably the cost is a higher rate of interest, usually around 15.6 to 16.95 per cent. And annual fees are also much higher than standard cards in exchange for an extensive range of extra features, such as hotel discounts to specialised customer reward programs. Some banks will waive the following year's fees if you spend over a certain amount.

The National Bank, for example, will waive the fees on its gold Visa or Mastercard if spending exceeds $8000 and $15 000 respectively.

One card is enough

It seemed like good news when the American Express company offered a new kind of credit card to its members last year. Until then Amex has always insisted on payment in full at the end of the month. Now it is offering an additional card, operating a separate account which members can pay off on the drip.

But do we really need another card, I hear you asking? Well, here might be an example of a card that really is useful. For one thing members get a 14.55 per cent interest rate, about two percentage points lower than most of the competition, and there are up to 55 interest-free days on the account. As part of a money management plan, one type of card, say a Visa or Mastercard, could be used for supermarket purchases or ATM use, and another, say the new Amex credit card, for major items like a new computer or camera.

Remember, banks are in the business of lending, not advising their customers on how to handle their money. The pressure is relentless on consumers to *buy, buy, buy* on credit; they are being seduced into purchasing whatever they want whenever they want it. Horror stories abound.

The hardest thing for a parent is to say no to their children. And Janice wanted the best for her kids. Being a working mum, she left the three-year old at day care and the five-year old at kindergarten. And having moved interstate with her mining engineer husband, she relied a lot on the network of parents from both child-minding centres.

Regular visits to the local shopping centre was an outing for Janice and her children and an outlet for her pressured life. And kids being kids, they always wanted the brightest and the best. Janice bought them little gifts for their birthdays. 'It's so hard to say no.'

She bought on credit, using both her Bankcard and her Visa card. And while she had always paid the minimum amount due on each card, she found the debts gradually mounting.

Within nine months of moving, Janice found that she could no longer afford day care fees. She had fallen a month behind and the owners of the centre denied her further access. She was humiliated and too embarrassed to confront her husband. She changed her working hours at the travel agency where she worked as a commission-based consultant to accommodate a child at home, but found it impossible to maintain an income.

She was forced to give up work, telling her husband that she wanted to look after the infant as a full-time mum. Meanwhile, thousands of dollars in credit card debts were accumulating interest and now, even the minimum monthly payments could not be met.

'I'd always hoped that I'd find the money somehow.' Janice fell into a deep depression and sought medical treatment. Fortunately the counsellor advised that she cut and burn all her credit cards, suggesting also that she contact her creditors immediately.

At some point in our lives we have all suffered some of Janice's excesses.

Cutting costs to the bone

Chris Gosselin claims that many people have learned to use credit cards *properly*. 'Around 36 per cent of credit card users manage to pay no interest. That is, they pay the debit off in full each month and then use the credit period of 52 days effectively. It's a very good way to run your credit card.'

We all have someone in the family — an aunt or distant relative — that has turned the art of frugality into fortune. You know the type — they know the best times to phone interstate and they know the cheapest brand of dried apricots on the supermarket shelf. I couldn't resist asking aunt Molly what credit cards she used.

'Let me tell you this, young man. If you're really serious about saving money, take out a pair of scissors and cut them in two.'

I had already decided that Molly was a bit of a dinosaur, thinking she saw cards and electronic banking as having passed her by — a modern *fad*. But to my amazement she rattled on: 'If you need a card for emergencies keep one and have its credit limit reduced to $1000. If you're always in debt to the tune of $1000 or more you haven't got a savings problem, you've got a spending problem! And make sure you don't pay those rotten banks a cent of your hard-earned money.

'No fees and no interest. Pay off your account every month. I have a Metway Visa credit card because they charge no fees and I get 30 interest-free days and they have a 12.95 per cent interest rate.

Remember that: no fees and no interest!'

I quickly calculated that my Bankcard was charging interest at a whopping 4 per cent more than aunt Molly's. I always knew Molly had to be listened to. But Molly was not finished with me yet…

'And don't use a credit card which is linked to a bank account for ordinary shopping. Those banks will charge you for the transaction just as if it was a cheque. Pay in cash.'

Molly had spoken. I felt uneasy, not only because I knew I was paying nearly 17 per cent interest on my credit card, 5 per cent more than Molly, but also because I knew it was impossible for me to pay off my credit card every single month. We've already noted it takes months to recover (financially) from the festive season.

Paying in cash?

Seems like an anachronism, doesn't it? Have we really been brain-washed to the extent that we now perceive cash as irrelevant and dated?

Suppose you want to buy a new computer for $2900 and you don't have the money in the bank to pay cash; so you put it on your credit card. The credit card facility is charging interest of 16.95 per cent, but you continue to pay the minimum monthly balance of around $150. At this rate, it will take you around three years to pay for the computer because you will not only be paying the monthly balance but interest as well. You are paying interest on interest! In fact, a total interest bill of around $900, making the total cost of your new computer $3800.

Everyone loves a bargain. And there are bargains to be had. But *not* with a credit card. Remember the retailer has to pay his merchant's fees, generally up to 5 per cent of the sale price, to the credit card companies and banks. While this is not a lot, you might be surprised just how much you save if you do offer cash.

Asking retailers if they will give you a discount for buying with cash is often very effective. I tested this theory when I wanted to buy a computer. A privately owned dealership in Brookvale, Sydney, offered me a 5 per cent discount for a cash deal. I was offered the computer in the above example for $2755.

The comparison between cash and a credit card purchase is revealing. In this example the difference is more than $1000!

Or expressed in interest rate terms, you are paying an effective rate of more than 20 per cent per annum on your credit card purchase when compared with a cash transaction. Had you saved for that computer purchase you would have earned extra interest on your interest-bearing account.

Credit cards are only of real *value* in an emergency situation where you need money immediately and you know you can pay the amount back within the interest-free period. Sure, they are convenient, and easy credit is always a temptation. For those on a strict budget, credit card usage is expensive and can lead to the unwanted debt cycle covered earlier in this chapter.

Tip-offs to rip-offs

- Pay as much off your credit card as you can: a regular amount each month — such debts just don't go away.
- Don't use more than one credit card.
- Replace high interest credit cards with low interest credit cards. For example, throw away store cards that charge excessive rates.
- If you use your credit card for cash advances remember that the 55-day interest-free period does not apply.
- Treat your credit card exactly the same way you would your own money. Don't buy things you wouldn't otherwise buy — if you buy on credit the money to repay the debt doesn't fall out of the sky.
- Don't carry credit cards because you think they're more secure than cash — use debit cards instead. They're just like credit cards except they don't get you into debt.

Chapter 10

Your credit rating: does it matter?

Rob, a professional and recently divorced, gave his wife a generous settlement, including full ownership of the matrimonial home, leaving himself with little by way of assets. He had an unblemished record of meeting all his loan obligations with banks and other financial institutions. He also had a small overdraft on his transaction account at the bank.

Not long after the divorce settlement he received notice from his bank demanding clearance of his overdraft in full and forthwith. His only means of raising the funds was by drawing cash to the limit on two of his credit cards. Things then took a turn for the worse.

He fell ill and was forced to take leave for six weeks — without pay. By the second month he'd failed to meet the minimum due payments on his credit cards and letters of demand were made on him. Several months later both debts were in the hands of collection agencies and he was forced to go through the humiliating task of negotiating small monthly payments to repay the debts — now totally nearly $10 000.

More than 18 months later, after saving some money, he approached a building society to seek a loan for a home he wanted to purchase. His application was refused — both credit card issuers and his bank had earlier referred him to the Credit Reference Association of Australia (CRAA). He was now considered a poor credit risk.

Apart from the unconscionable conduct of the bank, Rob's mistake was not so much a case of over-commitment but of failing to advise his lenders of changed circumstances, leaving them no choice but to take action and to press for a resolution.

By referring his name to the CRAA the money lenders were only doing their job. (Incidentally, a record of illness at the CRAA would go a long way towards explaining any credit problems.) Rob now had a stained credit record and was to suffer from this for a number of years.

Many of our 'horror' stories have sadly ended with the ruination of a person's credit rating, all too often stemming from some foul up by the bank. And while this is not a common outcome, it is important to consider what a credit rating means in today's debt-laden society.

The chapter will outline what you need to know about your credit rating and how to ensure you keep an unblemished record.

What is a credit rating?

If you are steadily employed and you manage your finances sensibly, you probably devote as much time thinking about your credit rating as you do your car's spare tyre. But you may need it unexpectedly — in applying for a credit card, for raising the limits on an existing one, or when applying for a personal loan or mortgage. It's up to you to make sure your credit rating provides potential creditors with no reason to question your credit worthiness.

A credit rating is essentially the record of your past performance in paying your bills. Although individuals don't get tagged with a credit rating in the same way as, for example, a corporation would, we do, in Australia have a sophisticated credit reporting system. The most significant and largest centralised agency, with over nine million files, is the Credit Reference Association of Australia Limited, commonly referred to as the CRAA.

Each day tens of thousands of people who apply for credit end up on record at the CRAA (the CRAA receives six million enquires a year). This is irrespective of whether or not the application was approved and irrespective of whether or not any particular person had defaulted on a prior debt. The enquires are received from its 4500 members who include banks, finance companies, department stores, public utilities such as Telstra, and the Gas and Fuel Corporation, motor car traders, real estate agents, building societies and credit unions.

A typical CRAA file (see example pages 199–200) will list a number of identity details (for example, date of birth and address) — enough to correctly identify you should it receive an inquiry about you from a credit supplier. CRAA records are not unlike a diary of events in a consumer's life.

An important part of the CRAA file is the default reports the Association receives from its members. These typically cover people who have been subject to collection actions for non-payment of accounts or who have had a motor vehicle repossessed or who have left their addresses to avoid creditors.

It is up to the lender to advise the CRAA on any incident that, in its opinion, warrants a notification to the CRAA. It is unlikely, for example, that forgetting to pay your monthly

CRAA CREDIT REFERENCE ASSOCIATION OF AUSTRALIA LIMITED A.C.N. 000 602 862

Public Access Division

Level 5, 90 Arthur Street, North Sydney, NSW 2060
PO Box 964, North Sydney, NSW 2059
Tel 1 300 364 141

Individual Credit Report

Ms S Rose-Watkins
5/32 Derma Ave
Cabramatta
NSW 2166

Your ref
PAS 9406

Dear Ms S Rose-Watkins,

Thank you for your request for a copy of your credit information file.

Credit Reference Association of Australia is a not-for-profit organisation owned by its members such as banks, finance companies, credit unions and department stores.

CRAA's main service to its members is that of a credit reporting agency.

We maintain credit information for five years from the date of placement. Once this time period has expired the data is automatically removed from the database.

These purge rules are in compliance with the Privacy Amendment Act 1990 which governs an individual's consumer credit file.

Identity Details:

Name:	SANDRA ROSE-WATKINS
Date of Birth:	5/12/46
Sex:	Female

Including your current address, we have the following address history on file.

65 RAYNOR Avenue DENISTONE NSW 2114
5 / 32 DERRNA Avenue CABRAMATTA NSW 2166

Employment Details:

Your last known employment as reported to us was with ROSIES ROSES P/L as a DIRECTOR.

Name Cross Reference:

The following are other names by which you have been made known to us by our members.

SANDRA WATKINS

CREDIT REFERENCE ASSOCIATION OF AUSTRALIA LIMITED
ACN 000 602 862

PUBLIC ACCESS DIVISION PAS 9406

Consumer Credit Information

Information in your consumer credit file is obtained from credit providers who are members of the Association. This file contains information about applications for a loan sought which is intended for domestic, family or household purposes.

Credit applications:

These are enquiries made by credit providers resulting from applications for credit made by you, whether or not you proceeded with your application.

COMMONWEALTH BANK LOAN CTR Q made an enquiry on 14/9/93 in reference to an application for a Chattel Mortgage account where you applied as a Joint applicant for the amount of $5,000.

ALL SBURBS VIDEO RENTALS NSW made an enquiry on 3/1/92 in reference to an application for a Rental account where you applied as a Guarantor for the amount of $435.

Overdue Account(s):

These are accounts that are reported to us as being more than 60 days in arrears.

On 19/3/95 ARFN TARGET CARD VIC advised that a Continuing Credit account reference 1234 was overdue. They reported the amount overdue as $1,234, due to a payment default.

On 22/5/96 it was advised that this account has been settled.

On 20/1/93 WESTPAC 341 GEORGE ST NSW advised that a Loan Contract account reference 039422 was overdue. They reported the amount overdue as $1,234, due to a payment default.

On 3/9/95 it was advised that this account is under dispute.

Please note: *Overdue accounts which were listed prior to 25th February 1992 may need to be verified with the credit provider.*

File Notes:

These notes provide additional information about the contents of your file.

29/11/95 *** THIS IS A TEST FILE ***

File Access

This list is for your information only and is not viewed by members of the Association. It is a record of organisations that have been given access to your credit information file.

18/12/96 CRAA PUBLIC ACCESS DIVISION.
29/11/95 CRAA PUBLIC ACCESS DIVISION.

instalment on your monthly repayment schedule for your car would be referred to the CRAA. But, if you have defaulted on an agreement, where, for example, the lender has attempted to recover a debt from you legally, then it is very likely that you would be referred to the CRAA and that a record would exist against your name for failing to meet your obligations on a loan agreement. The amount in question is also noted and the lending organisation is named. Details remain on your file for five years or seven in the case of bankruptcy.

Disputes with the bank

A dispute with a bank may or may not result in a referral to the CRAA. Any dispute with a lender — bank or otherwise — should be checked out. You would need to apply in writing for a copy of your record. Should any disputed matter be on your file, you are quite entitled to request that your side of the story be entered on file against your name. So, even if the dispute was not resolved, there may still be grounds for entering your story. Of particular importance here is any documentation from the Banking Ombudsman that relates to your particular dispute (see next chapter). This is, once again, an illustration of the importance of maintaining written records, documents and diary notes of conversations. Don't end up with a negative record at the CRAA for no wrongdoing on your part.

Where, for example, a person fails to make payments to a bank on a particular agreement because he or she has an issue with the bank about overcharging or incorrect fees, and this results in a broader dispute, this should not affect their credit rating if there are legitimate grounds for the dispute. Once again, the Banking Ombudsman can play a role, and the matter needs to be referred to the Ombudsman.

Incidentally, with regard to credit listing, the Privacy Act requires that a payment be at least 60 days overdue before a default can be recorded. Watch the banks here, as there are numerous incidents noted by the Office of the Ombudsman of banks prematurely listing payment defaults.

You keep control — it's your life

Your record should be reviewed (by yourself) regularly. The CRAA will provide a copy of your report free of charge, together with a simple explanation of how to read it. There are factors to consider when checking your report:

- Accuracy. Because credit bureau reports are computerised, errors that a human would detect may pass unnoticed to your permanent record.
- A bill you may have legitimately refused to pay because of a dispute over the quality of the goods or services you purchased may be improperly reported to the credit bureau as a non-payment.

The information most likely to appear on your report comes from bank cards such as Master Card or Visa; charge accounts at department stores such as Myer or David Jones; and some travel and entertainment cards such as Diners Club.

A spokesperson for the CRAA advised me that while the majority of people handle their financial affairs responsibly, resulting in a *clean* record, many people get into difficulties on a variety of loans ranging from credit cards, hire purchase agreements and commercial disputes between business people and their suppliers and creditors.

Your file at the CRAA does not show how much you have borrowed, or your current credit commitments. Nor does it show other personal data such as your religion, salary, record of parking infringements or criminal record (if any). It should *only* show the amount you have defaulted on and with whom.

It does not matter, therefore, if you have more debts than assets, or whether you have one or ten different lenders, provided you do not significantly fall into arrears on any repayments, prompting legal recovery action by a lender.

Establishing a good credit rating

The first principle of establishing a good credit rating or, at least avoiding a bad one, is not to default on any loan. It is very important to advise, in writing, any lender of any circumstances which might interfere with the smooth flow of your repayments.

Most lenders — banks or other lending institutions — will accommodate any reasonable request for altering repayments — either by granting a temporary respite (terms by mutual agreement) or a smaller amount (again by mutual agreement). And even in the case of total financial collapse, where you can't even see the possibility of repayment, it is still worth maintaining a dialogue. Failure to keep your lender informed could result in a referral to the CRAA.

In the case of a negative referral it would be very difficult to raise even the smallest amounts of credit, or apply for a new credit card, for example. And the situation could prevail for years until the records are set straight — usually by repayment of the debt or some agreed settlement. And if this occurs at a young age it could jeopardise your chances of qualifying for a home loan later on as a married person.

Positive credit reporting — where every person, not just those with a poor credit history, gets a credit rating — will soon become the norm. Positive credit reporting will make it possible to negotiate discounts on, for example, home loans. The Commonwealth Bank already offers home loan discounts of up to 0.5 percentage points to members of some professional bodies.

If you are at fault

An unfavourable credit report is relatively easy to correct if the credit bureau or creditor has made an error. But if you are at fault — by having been delinquent on your payments, for example — the process may be more difficult. In that case you have two options:

- If you have paid the overdue amount you can ask the creditor to advise the credit bureau that your debt has been cleared.
- You are entitled by law to write a comment explaining the reason for your delinquency. This comment, which will appear on your credit report in the future, should offer an explanation that is likely to be acceptable to any intending creditor: loss of job, for example, or business failure, illness or a death in the family.

If you are applying for credit, offering an explanation in advance or forewarning your creditor about past problems may offset his or her negative reaction to your unfavourable credit report. This may be an uncomfortable position for most, but, where the record is already blemished, there is nothing to lose.

It should be remembered that there are many other reasons why you could lawfully be denied credit:

- temporary or irregular employment
- inability to verify employment
- length of employment is too short
- insufficient income
- excessive obligations
- inability to verify income
- too short a period of residence
- temporary residence

- no credit file; that is, no record of ever having established a loan
- bankruptcy.

How to use your bank

A more effective way to enjoy credit when your rating is poor is to obtain a charge card or debit card or a secured credit card from a bank. Under this arrangement you deposit a certain amount of money in the bank as a form of collateral and are issued a card with a line of credit not exceeding the amount you have on deposit.

A good credit rating is mainly about meeting your commitments and maintaining a scrupulous relationship with your lenders. It is also about good borrowing practice. And good borrowing practice is all about doing your homework in regard to the loan application.

It generally doesn't pay to exaggerate income or assets, because if you don't qualify for a loan in your current circumstances, guess what? The lender is probably convinced you can't afford the repayments. And attempting to squeeze through the cracks could result in a negative record at the CRAA, rendering all future loan applications futile.

In terms of getting a loan from the bank — say, a personal loan without any equity in a property — having a *nil* record at the CRAA is not necessarily to your advantage. In fact, with no record of your name at the CRAA a lender may be disinclined to grant you a loan simply on the grounds that you have no track record of ever having paid back a loan!

My advice to first-time borrowers is to seek finance from a credit union, after first having maintained a track record of savings at a bank or credit union. You may even be able to score a written statement from your bank manger at the local branch that you maintained such an account and that you deposited regular amounts each and every month and at all times maintained a credit balance.

You may also have taken out life or disability insurance requiring regular payments. A written record from the life insurance company could also come in handy. If you have private medical insurance, this too will form a basis for a good credit rating. If you have ever worked as an independent contractor or have bought things on credit from the local hardware supplier or even the local newsagent, you could, with a bit of arm twisting, get them to sign a statement (write it yourself and ask them to sign or copy onto their letterhead).

These small businesses tend not to check the CRAA, so opening up an account with them will assist in you building your own *triple A* credit rating.

Armed with all this you could ask for a personal loan. As a final fall-back, if the credit union or bank will not or cannot offer you an unsecured personal loan, ask whether a guarantee from another person will assist in a successful application. This is another avenue to explore with friends or family.

How to develop your own powerful credit profile

Your credit profile will determine how easy or difficult it is to get bank loans, credit cards, or any other form of financing. In some cases it may even influence whether you get a certain job or an insurance policy. A positive credit profile does its own explaining so that you don't have to. The elements of a powerful credit profile are:

- a positive up-to-date CRAA report
- a home with a mortgage
- an American Express or Diners Club card
- a job you've held for a year or more

- a current or paid-off bank loan
- a Master or Visa card
- a department store credit card
- a telephone account in your name.

There is some order of importance intended here. Clearly it is much more advantageous to own a home (with mortgage) than to hold a mobile phone account. Owning a home with a mortgage shows stability and can swing you into a powerful credit profile position.

As a principle, it would seem self evident that the greater the number of loans you run simultaneously, the higher the chances that you will end up in difficulty with one or more, thus running the real risk of staining your credit record. What is intended here should not be mistaken for reckless opening up of debt on a number of fronts.

The reason American Express and Diners cards have clout is that you need to demonstrate to the providers of credit that you are on a certain minimum income, and have paid the balance of your accounts with them each month — again a sign of credit worthiness.

- Above all be prepared to go public with your information in order to further your credit profile. This may, at times, involve providing information such as tax returns, as well as your CRAA report.
- Obtain a report from your bank manager, based on a minimum level of savings, good transaction account behaviour (no bounced cheques!) and any bank loans that have been paid off.

Remember that many banks usually approve an application for credit based on a points system, with points assigned from different categories. Most of the categories they would use would be included in the earlier list.

Also, remember your CRAA files contains:

- all previous credit applications — even the ones that don't go through
- all defaults — even after they've been repaid.

However there is a time limit to information being held and after this limit it must be destroyed.

Check list

- Check your credit report.
- Ensure all credit you use is reported in your given name and surname: 'Bill Citizen', not 'Mr Bill Citizen'. (Yes, it is possible that two files could exist.)
- Obtain at least one bank card (Master Card or Visa) in your own name (as above).
- If you are not married but plan to marry in the future, consider leaving your credit card in your own last name because many women discover that linking their financial identity to that of their husband leads to trouble later.
- If you are married now but your marriage is not secure, consider building a separate credit identity in your birth name now. The law provides for your right to credit in your birth name if you so choose, and having credit of your own will make separation or divorce, if necessary, easier.

There are traps for the unwary. Having a *record* at the CRAA will cost you in terms of availability of cheaper forms of credit. Establishing a powerful credit profile can save money. For example, nearly every department store offer for interest-free loans and no payments 6 months' style specials are fraught with expensive financing for the unwary buyer. In nearly all cases it would be preferable — if you really want the product

— to shop around for your own loan. These companies tend to lend to higher risk borrowers and charge more. Similarly, in the case of motor vehicle dealers, you can be certain that the finance they offer is expensive. Dealers often have to deal with less-than-credit-worthy people.

If you have a good credit rating you don't need to pay this extra interest cost, which is likely to be higher by several percentage points, at least.

Tips

- *If you are young* and have not yet operated on credit (e.g. plastic or personal loan) open accounts at a bank and, for example, a health fund or local store to establish a track record of good credit habits.
- *Never use mortgage grace periods.* Don't be late with your mortgage repayments. Even though most banks allow a grace period (usually around 10 days) before they will charge a late penalty, a late payment could end up on your CRAA file.
- When you are short of cash, *paying the minimum due on your bills* — especially credit cards — should receive top priority so that you can preserve your credit rating. If there is no minimum due and you are dealing with a bank or other financial institution, make some payment with an explanatory note. Even under the most dire consequences, if you are considered as defaulting on your repayment, your note can appear on your file. *Above all, communicate with your lender at the first sign of trouble.*

Chapter 11

Disputes with your bank: what to do

You've just replaced that leaky hot water service and bang, it blows a seal. Your new kitchen whiz goes berserk and you put in a complaint to one of the States' Fair Trading departments, and the department will probably spring into action, investigate the complaint and arrange a remedy.

However, if you have a dispute with the bank chances are that not only will the government department not help you but you will need to go through some fairly tortuous steps to get your dispute resolved. If you are a normal consumer of bank services the Banking Ombudsman's office is available as a resource, but, unfortunately, if you are a small business person, trading as a sole trader, a partnership or a company, you may find yourself falling through the cracks of the system and not having anywhere to turn.

In this chapter we will follow the steps necessary to get your dispute with the bank resolved. There are also some basic habits that you need to get into to always maximise your position because banks do not have a good record in acting in the customer's best interest.

Peter Kell of the Australian Consumers' Association reckons that the Australian financial services sector — of which banks represent the largest component — has a very poor record of complaints handling. So what can you do if your bank gives you misleading information, bad service or you disagree with your account records?

'Consumers don't just complain about bank charges,' says Peter Kell. 'They also complain about service. They just don't get the service they deserve any more. Banking today is technology driven and the people in the front line of the bank — at the counters — are not trained to deal with customers' problems. They just push the paperwork.

'The problem is deep-rooted. The finance sector has a very poor record in customer service. People coming into the bank with problems or complaints today don't get any satisfaction. They are often greeted with a shrug or a glib answer that "it's all in the small print".'

According to Peter Kell, 'If you don't complain, the banks will never change.'

In the first instance you should always take up the complaint with the bank, which should have a clearly set-out complaints resolution process that should be available.

Get it in writing must be one of the oldest rules in the book, but in personal banking it is still easier said than done. And, if you can't get it in writing from the bank, putting it in your own writing is definitely better than nothing.

After a lifetime of pondering the problem, John Reynolds has finally learned how to do business with banks.

'I've dealt with them all around the world. Nearly all of them at times have shown ineptness, ignorance and incompetence. You must be absolutely specific with every instruction, as if communicating with a simple child.

'One must be firm to the point of aggression and even mistrustful. You need to document all conversations with the bank, preferably in your diary, something like this:

"9 August: Spoke to Mr Scrooge about interest charges on my overdraft. He said he'd investigate and get back to me. I asked when I could expect a response. He indicated sometime later in the week.

"16 August: Spoke to Mr Scrooge about interest charges again. He advised that bank had checked figures and said that there was no discrepancy to the original amount. I asked what amount he'd arrived at, to which he replied that he didn't have the file in front of him. I asked whether he would be prepared to put in writing the results of his investigation. He said yes.

"25 August: Spoke to Mr Scrooge again. He apologised for not writing but he's had staff problems. I suggested that my patience was wearing thin and that my next move would be to refer the matter to the Banking Ombudsman.

"28 August: Letter arrives from the bank. No details of interest calculations. No amount quoted.

"29 August. Spoke to the Banking Ombudsman spokesperson, who listened to my complaint and asked me to submit my file, including my diary notes, with a covering letter to her office."'

According to a retired senior banker the heart of the problem is communications — or a lack of it. 'You must talk a language that the bankers understand. What this means for most consumers is an ability to get into facts, actual records and conversation, not just vague recollections.'

The Banking industry ombudsman: how to lodge a complaint

If a complaint to the bank doesn't bring satisfaction, which it clearly didn't in John Reynold's case, the Australian Banking Industry Ombudsman (ABIO) may be the next call. The ABIO is a free complaints resolution scheme, with the first point of contact usually the phone.

A spokesperson for the ABIO noted that the profile of the average enquirer is skewed towards high income earners. This probably meant that there were many people who were not aware of the service and who therefore had no ability to resolve their queries or complaints other than with the bank concerned.

Problems associated with transactions and calculations continued to be the main problem addressed to the Banking Ombudsman, accounting for more than 24 per cent of complaints received by the ABIO. For most of 1996, telephone enquires averaged more than 7000 per month.

Office staff provided consumers with advice concerning bank-related problems. Initially, officers referred callers to key customer relations staff at the member bank concerned, so that bank management could respond directly to their customers.

Telephone callers who remain dissatisfied after contacting their bank directly are invited to formalise their grievances to the ABIO in writing.

To assist a caller who may have difficulties in submitting a written complaint an enquiries officer fills out a pro forma complaint form which details the complaint provided by the consumer over the telephone. The form is sent to the consumer for verification before the enquiries officer refers it to the bank.

If the complaint falls within the scheme's jurisdiction, enquiries officers send a copy of the consumer's complaint to the bank's senior management and encourage the consumer

How complaints are resolved

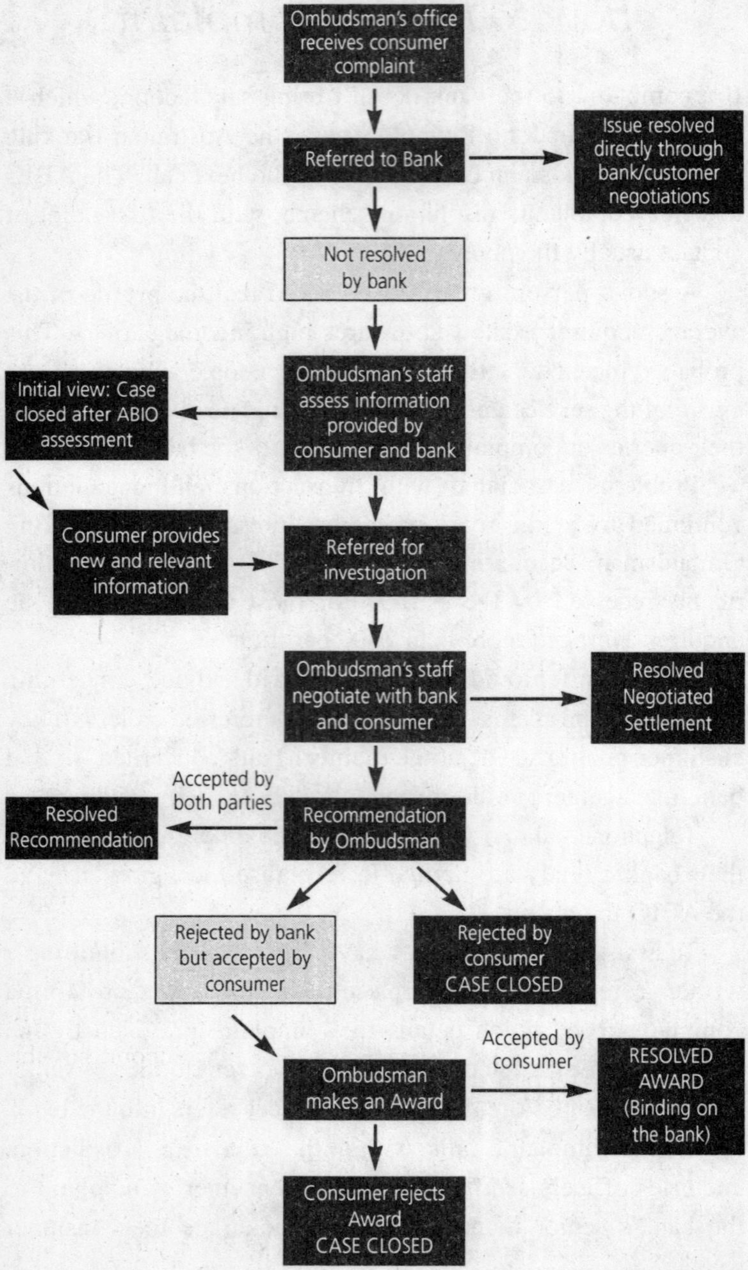

and the bank to negotiate. Enquiries officers ask the bank to report back to the ABIO within 30 days. At this stage resolution can take place and the file is be closed.

If the complaint remains unresolved enquires officers assess the information provided by the consumer and bank, and may seek an opinion from the Ombudsman's banking and legal advisers. Referral to a case manger for investigation usually occurs at this stage. However, if it appears from the information available that the bank's actions were reasonable, enquires officers advise the consumer of their initial view in writing.

This initial view often satisfies the consumer by providing an independent assessment of the bank's actions. However, it also gives consumers the opportunity to have their complaint investigated further if they can show there are still unresolved issues or if they can identify factual inaccuracies.

The next step in the complaint resolution process ensures that a consumer's dispute is independently assessed when a deadlock has been reached between bank and consumer. Case managers reconstruct the sequence of events, collect statements from both parties, examine the bank's customer file and obtain legal opinion where appropriate, together with advice from the Ombudsman's independent adviser on banking practice.

The case manager's findings, including a clear explanation of the reason for the decision, are provided to the bank and the consumer. If the case manager finds that the information does not support the consumer's claim, the consumer is asked to withdraw the complaint. If the investigation reveals the bank does have a case to answer the case manager encourages the bank to take appropriate action to settle the dispute, which may involve compensation for financial loss.

Some complaints are resolved through what is called a conciliation conference. This informal conference brings both parties together to discuss the matter on neutral ground at a venue convenient to the consumer. (Many bank customers have a genuine anxiety about sitting near an authority figure such as a bank manager.) After exploring the facts and issues at the conference, if both parties agree to a resolution, the Ombudsman will confirm the negotiated settlement reached in writing.

If a case manager cannot settle the complaint at the negotiated settlement stage the Ombudsman considers the results of the investigation and issues a recommendation. The recommendation takes into account, among other things, any new information provided by the consumer or bank to support their case. If the information provided does not support the consumer's case, the Ombudsman recommends that that the consumer withdraw the complaint. The consumer is then advised that the Office is unable to assist any further and the file is closed.

If the Ombudsman makes a recommendation that the bank compensates the consumer for financial loss and both parties accept it, the dispute is resolved and the file is closed.

When the consumer rejects the recommendation and the bank accepts it, the consumer is told that the Office is unable to assist them further and the file is closed.

Where the Ombudsman makes a recommendation that the bank compensates a consumer for financial loss, which the consumer accepts but the bank rejects, the Ombudsman makes an award. Once given by the Ombudsman, the award is binding on the bank if accepted by the consumer.

Resolution does not always mean complete compensation. Take, for example, this case from the ABIO's own files:

Mr G told the bank to cancel debits from his savings account to his health insurance fund. Payments continued and after eight months the consumer raised the matter with the bank. Mr G was advised that he would need to contact the health fund to cancel the direct debit authority. Mr

G complained that if the bank had given him the advice eight months earlier he would have saved $700 in payments.

After intervention by the ABIO, the bank refunded two payments of $265.85 and the consumer accepted this in resolution of his complaint.

Why did Mr G accept only a part refund? Consumers of bank services often feel powerless. The ABIO scheme goes a long way to redress this. Although the complaints resolution process is time consuming and, by nature, often drawn out, genuine grievances do find willing ears.

Does this system really work?

Research has shown that only one in seven Australians who had a concern about a banking service raised the matter with his or her bank before changing financial institutions. People just throw their hands to the air in despair and either do nothing or move on to another bank or, in many cases, a building society or other non-bank enterprise.

Research also shows that a large proportion of respondents (46 per cent) made two or three attempts to resolve the matter with only 39 per cent of these concerns being satisfied. By the time these consumers sought ABIO intervention they had made, on average, *six* or *seven* attempts to resolve their grievances without success.

What is really disturbing is that if a bank fails to resolve a matter to the consumer's satisfaction then, under the Code of Banking Practice, which came into force during 1995–96, the bank should inform consumers of their right to raise their concerns with the Ombudsman. But only about 17 per cent of consumers who complained to their bank were informed of the Ombudsman's existence by bank staff. Now banks are required to publish a disputes resolution statement on all their product and service brochures.

The scheme is not elitist and the profile of the typical scheme user suggests that although higher income people and white-collar workers are over-represented, the scheme is used by people from all walks of life. However, there are limits to the types of complaints the Ombudsman can consider:

- a claim for a loss of more than $150 000
- problems that arise from incorporated (Pty Ltd) companies
- matters involving the commercial judgment of the bank, such as whether a loan is granted
- matters involving a bank's general interest rate policy or practice.

Thus contractual issues, delays, lost funds, fees and charges, withdrawal or deposit errors are some of the problems that the Ombudsman can help with. Over 125 000 people have (since January 1990) telephoned the office of the Ombudsman to inquire about their banking problems and 18 000 letters from people across Australia have asked the office to investigate their complaints. At the end of 1995, 88 per cent of written complaints had been resolved to the customer's satisfaction.

In some cases resolution may not have involved financial compensation but, for example, restructuring a customer's loan, having bank charges waived, or customers may have received a full and clear explanation of the events that led to their complaint arising, which was enough to satisfy their unease.

My own experience and anecdotal evidence suggests that merely threatening to inform the Ombudsman of any substantial grievance, will often produce the desired outcome. (Unfortunately, waiting in a queue at the bank while your car is booked by a traffic policeman for standing in a bus zone is not a matter for the Ombudsman.)

And while the ABIO process is quicker and easier than any alternative, it can take a long time. The Ombudsman's report reveals that it takes *201* days to resolve an investigation (based on the average length of a case). Courts and tribunals can take much longer to sort out your problem and can be very costly. Also, you lose none of your legal rights by bringing a complaint to the Ombudsman.

Commercial disputes

If you're in business and you can't take your case to the Ombudsman, then what are the alternatives to having your dispute with the bank resolved? If all negotiations with the bank have ceased, then legal recourse may be the only means. Unfortunately, the bank may have already instituted its own legal proceedings by this stage.

You need to seek legal advice if you are already or soon to be in default of your mortgage, for example. You will need to collate all documents, letters, contracts, bank statements etc. in date order and write a very detailed account of what happened quoting dates, times, places and conversations.

If you are in a position of strong defence why wait until the bank takes you to court? And although you must be prepared to go to court with well-prepared documentation, it must be remembered that litigation is a costly exercise for all parties and therefore no one is ever a real winner.

Marsha Wajnsztajn of the Australians for Banking Justice claims that there are hundreds of millions of dollars worth of unresolved disputes between small business and the banks. 'Most problems arise because less than 30 per cent of customers will either not read or do not understand what they're signing. This leads to all sorts of problems. Banks profit from confusion.'

If you are a small to medium-sized business and you are having a dispute with your bank you must act decisively — it's possible the bank may trigger default mechanisms that will result in unnecessary and premature seizure of assets.

The small business complaints received by the banks fall into several categories. These include:

- overcharging interest: penalty interest rates and fees
- ambiguous or unclear documentation, or even tampering with it.

Unfortunately, the normal avenues for dispute resolution — that is, the Banking Ombudsman — is not available to the business person if the debt or consideration in dispute exceeds $150 000. Redress is effectively beyond most business consumers due to the cost and expense of litigation through progressively superior courts.

Marsha had experienced first hand the complaints of more than 350 business customers. Banks tend to go underground when confronted with a complaint from a business customer — particularly those where the bank has taken some kind of default action already.

'People have been stone-walled by the banks. Standard responses from them have been: "... we don't agree with your version of the events ...", "... if you believe you have a case, then you should take us to court ...", "... it's not for us to justify our actions, it's up to you to prove we're wrong and negligent' or "... prove it if you can ..."'

As a final note, there may be other avenues you can approach for assistance and advice. Small business people can contact the Chamber of Commerce or various industry associations.

Electronic banking: how to deal with problems

In the future, problems (and therefore potential disputes) will almost certainly mount as there will be a whole range of interactive banking services provided via telephones and home computers, including payments to third parties, information held by banks and cash withdrawals by smart cards.

With the explosion of telephone banking services comes the risk of disputes over who said what. It's important that the consumer takes diary notes of the conversation relating to any banking transaction for future reference should any dispute erupt.

That means noting the name of the operator, the time of the conversation, the transaction number and the gist of what was said. If the operator is unknown it will be almost impossible to track down.

Steps to resolve your dispute

The Consumer Credit Legal Centre represents a new avenue for dispute resolution. From the new Consumer Credit Code enacted last November consumers will for the first time have the right to claim over-commitment as a legal principle if they believe the lender should never have granted a problem loan in the first place. This would become very important if rates were ever to return to the very high levels of a few years ago.

The code brings the credit tribunal system into the centre stage of the dispute resolution process. James Hutchinson of the Consumer Credit Legal Centre, Sydney, says that this is an added benefit to consumers caught in a dispute or default situation with their lenders. 'Consumers should be aware that they don't have to simply lie down and accept poor banking practices.'

Existing borrowers can use the tribunal in addition to the Banking Ombudsman service.

With banks now facing the possibility of criminal sanctions if the code is broken by staff, banks have scurried to their corners to train staff on the new code.

Five-step plan to dispute resolution

1 *Prepare yourself.* Be clear about what you want the bank to do.
2 *Provide* the bank with any supporting documentation (including diary notes) which you feel may clarify the situation.
3 *Establish contact.* Contact the branch where your accounts are held or the branch/department which handled your transaction. A phone call may be all that is required to resolve it. If a staff member is handling your complaint without satisfaction ask to speak with the branch manager.
4 *Still not satisfied*? Put your complaint in writing. Note the details of your complaint and send this to the State Manager responsible for the branch where you bank.
5 *The Ombudsman.* If you feel your complaint has not been satisfactorily resolved you can seek further assistance from the ABIO. When you contact the office, give the full details of your complaint. Include:
   — your name, address and telephone number
   — the name of anyone who shares your bank accounts with you
   — what you think your bank has done wrong
   — how much you feel you have lost as a result of the problem
   —what you have already done to sort out the complaint with your bank.

Chapter 12

Small business needs

In late 1989 Glen and Iris saw a guest house in the southern highlands of NSW as a way of fulfilling their dream: running their own business in an idyllic holiday setting. But by the time it came to fruition the dream had turned into a nightmare.

'We approached the major banks and were told we didn't have enough equity', Glen recalls. 'So we kept trying. One friendly bank manager referred us to the bank-owned finance company where we obtained a loan.'

The first year went well but, as in all businesses, cash flow suffered interruptions — this is where the correct mix of debt to equity is critical.

Bookings fell away in Glen's and Iris's second year. They were forced to go cap-in-hand back to their bank manager for an overdraft.

'Interest rates were very high and because we were in a difficult situation, the bank loaded another couple of percentage points on to our lending rate. It forced us to lock in at these high rates just before interest rates started to fall. We were forced into part-time work just to support the loans,' Glen recalls.

As is often the case when adversity strikes, the couple found themselves in a debt trap. Their dream-turned-nightmare became unbearable and they had to sell. Interest charges and bank fees had all but eaten up their equity.

'Our first mistake was in plunging in with insufficient equity. We should have been alerted by the earlier rejections. Our second mistake was accepting a bank manager's advice on last-resort style financing. And the third mistake was in allowing ourselves to be locked in at high interest rates. We should have sought expert advice and not relied on the bank.' Glen and Iris are still regretting their business venture.

Debt traps for business

Unfortunately, for most small and medium-sized businesses debt is often the only means of financing business needs. Whether these needs are for new premises, stock or anything else, banks still remain the main source of loans, hence debt is the only path forward.

For most small business people the questions arise: Will the bank support me through my expansion? How can I avoid huge and unreasonable bank costs? What are my choices?

Have you ever wondered why banks charge anything up to 15 per cent interest and additional fees of thousands of dollars to businesses for an overdraft facility when that same bank may well be charging 8 or 9 per cent for money going to a home mortgage? This is a difference of 6 to 7 per cent! One business person I spoke to summed up what many have felt: 'You can't query bank charges because you're so heavily dependent on the bank. You just can't risk it.'

'There's no doubt that small business gets slugged by the banks harder and much more often than private customers,' says Peter Kell from the ACA, who sees this time and time again. 'The banks seem to be able to impose higher charges and more severe penalties on to the business customer with almost arrogant disregard. And there's no one out there to help them.'

One Tasmanian businessman queried the 35 miscellaneous bank charges on the three accounts he operated — the charges were all withdrawn because the bank could not justify or explain them.

'Business bank customers don't so much fall in between the cracks of the regulatory system as into huge chasms. And it's not just charges. The banks seem to put up every obstacle when they lend to small business.' Peter Kell cautions.

N wanted to set up practice as a counsellor in her home in Sydney's eastern suburbs. N owned her home outright — a neat bungalow conservatively valued at $400 000 — and had few debts other than an overdraft of a few thousand dollars, secured by her house deeds, and small credit card and charge card balances.

She had commenced private practice, borrowing rooms from colleagues to see private clients, but now wanted to set up a facility at home. N budgeted for $30 000 to tide her over until income from her practice could be built up, and for the necessary improvements that were needed to establish her rooms.

N presented a submission and previous years' tax returns to her bank. This is an extract of the reply she received:

'Unfortunately the Bank is unable to provide you further funds based on your stated income for 1996. It may now be best to sell your existing property ...'

In case you didn't notice, the bank suggested that N sell up her $400 000 home to raise $30 000!

A spokesperson for the bank confirmed that proposals such as this could fail on cash flow grounds, and also because of N's age (she was 50!). However, he did admit that an individual bank manager probably had the discretion to go either way in the matter. But, as every small business person knows, it takes time to build a business. It doesn't just kick off with the right numbers the day you start.

To rub salt into the wound, the manager later sent N another fax advising her that the interest rate on her current overdraft was to be reduced from 12.25 per cent to 11.75 per cent; all this at a time when banks were offering fixed rate home loans at 8.5 per cent!

Some weeks after this exchange N was still upset. 'She (the manager) made me feel like a leper. It was a humiliating experience.'

Please save us from the banks!

There is a great irony out there at the moment. Banks need small business — it remains one of the few areas of banking where they can return big margins and yet it is one of few remaining areas in banking where the banks make their customers — the small business person — still feel obligated to them.

'Embarrass the bastards'

Isaac had placed an ad in the newsletter of the Victims of the State Bank Association promoting the launch of his new Internet site under the banner 'Court judgements on the Internet'. It had the caption 'Have your judgement put on the Internet ... to show what the courts and banks are doing to us all'.

'I just want to embarrass the bastards,' Isaac Shields said when asked why he was placing a home page on the Internet.

Isaac had just lost a battle in the Federal Court against his bank. He was emphatic. 'Banks add layer upon layer of fees and then some more. But they make their real money from business accounts by liquidating them.'

Isaac, who had run a small engineering business with his wife on NSW's central coast, claims he ultimately lost his home and business and was not given any notice when the bank took possession of his home.

He alleges they sold everything. 'They sold the house for $124 000 when their own valuation three years earlier had it valued at $155 000.'

His experience in the courts is disturbing, and the documents available on the Internet site reveal a system which cares little for dispute resolution.

The case is a useful reminder of the often high stakes involved in the relationships between banks and small business. High stakes not only because of the personal exposure of many people in the volatile world of business, but because, unlike the private consumer, business customers often find themselves alone in the case of a dispute.

Unfortunately, apart from small sole traders, business borrowers cannot seek the help of the Bank Ombudsman if they suspect a mistake has been made in an overdraft or term loan account, for example. The Ombudsman's office cannot adjudicate business disputes (see Chapter 11).

Banks: a cause of business failure?

While loans to small and medium-sized businesses require much more complex risk assessment than for, say, home borrowers — which bankers would regard as a very safe bet — the huge gap in the interest charged to home borrowers compared with business borrowers begs for answers.

Shopping around and negotiating better deals are more important for small businesses. Unlike home loans, where banks can almost standardise the margins they apply because borrowers are fairly similar, small businesses present widely varying levels of risks to banks. Whereas the home lending market has witnessed the effects of competition, pushing interest rates down at least 2 percentage points, small business lending has, so far, missed out.

The banks are getting away with it because there is no free competition in the area of commercial banking. In almost every case, reductions in official interest rates have not been passed on immediately to customers. Banks withhold the reductions for as long as possible. After all, one half of one per cent on billions of dollars adds up each and everyday it is withheld.

Even in the area of home lending it took Aussie Home Loans to force banks to lower their interest rates by 1.75 per cent. But this was done in response to competition — and not by leading it!

There just isn't an Aussie Home Loans organisation around and, apart from the credit unions, there are few choices available to small businesses outside the banking industry. These are good reasons to not only shop around for the best deal but to watch and challenge existing charges very closely.

Interest rates: 'How to keep the bastards honest'

It is sad but true. Most business people don't know what they're being charged by the banks, either in fees or interest rates.

J had asked his bank to convert all his credit lines to bank bills since rates were coming down and he could save some interest. The bank tried to talk him out of it and even told him he was wrong. He finally showed them the sums and proved he was correct. Two weeks later he received word from head office that the bank had declined his request to convert because — wait for it — 'it was not in their interest to do so'!

If you're in business you need to be acutely aware of the costs of banking. Every business person would know that fees, charges and interest can eat up valuable cash flow. The following will give some pointers on what to look for in setting your business banking on cost-effective grounds.

Not content in dealing with the city office of his bank, Michael switched his business over to the local suburban branch, taking with him several business accounts, including a trust account and his personal accounts.

Michael had an overdraft facility on one of his business accounts secured by his home and knew the banks appreciated that his trust account always carried credit balances of many thousands of dollars — it was a sort of cash cow for the bank.

Michael was not very pleased when he was told he would have to renegotiate his line of credit with the new branch, knowing that this would inevitably cost. But he was downright annoyed when he was charged establishment fees and offered a facility with much stricter conditions than his former one.

'The new manager acknowledged that the trust account was a good account for the bank to have but I still had to front up to him with budgets and cash flows,' Michael recalled. 'I understand why a bank would do this for a new business customer but I'd been banking with this bank for ten years. I became very disillusioned.

'I felt the bank was getting the better of me in more ways than one. So I hired the services of a company that analyses a business's banking records over a specified period and recalculates the interest payments based on the bank's own information.'

According to one such bureau this is a growth industry due to the mistakes made by banks on an increasing scale. Roy Brown, a director of the Sydney-based Interest Research Bureau, claims that more than 90 per cent of his company's clients have experienced significant overcharging of interest by the banks. 'Discrepancies have been in the tens of thousands of dollars.'

In Michael's case, the discrepancy was found to be more than $2500 over a three-year period. His bureau completed a report on *variances and discrepancies* in the interest charged by the bank, and, armed with the report, Michael approached his bank manager. The bank manager — you guessed it — claimed it was not their mistake as his branch had only held the account for a few weeks.

Michael restructured his business finances, resulting in virtually no funds being left idle in cheque or low interest-paying accounts. Armed with a new determination to beat the banks Michael applied a more rigorous control of his outstanding debtors which allowed him to operate without the need for an overdraft facility.

'I don't know how much I've saved and that's bad enough isn't it? But I guess it would run into thousands of dollars every year. I got my $2500 back from them and an extra $300 thrown in for good measure for lost interest.'

How many business owners check their interest rate charges? While tedious, this calculation is not beyond most people and not that much different from, say, a stock-take. Roy Brown believes that there is more than just laziness involved. 'Many small business operators have developed an attitude where they believed they had to go cap-in-hand to the banks to get loans.'

Unfortunately, the margin for error is just too large, and with business owners already being slugged with rates 5 or 6 percentage points greater than home lending rates, no one can afford such laziness. Roy Brown claims that the main areas of error are the applications of incorrect interest rates by the banks.

Working out what you are being charged in interest is not everybody's favourite pastime, but it's the only way to 'keep the bastards honest,' says Roy Brown. If you find the idea of bringing in one of the investigative services mentioned above uncomfortable or cost prohibitive, then do it yourself.

All you do is multiply your daily interest rate by your daily overdraft balances for the period to the latest interest charge and sum the totals — if your grand total is significantly lower than what you've been charged, query it.

In my research for this book I've asked a number of small business people whether they've done this simple exercise. Not one had. And so they're all at the mercy of their lenders.

There are other concerns for small business people to be aware of:

- unexpected *extra* charges
- the default provisions of the loan agreement.

It has been a notable feature of published bank rates that they speak in terms of *base rate*. What matters is the *actual* rate. You can always check the newspapers for the base rate. In this way you can regain some control by asking the bank if the rate appears excessive.

Tip: Before you sign anything determine what rate of interest you will be charged and insist on being advised promptly every time this rate is to be changed.

This margin over the base rate is *definitely* negotiable, and if your bank attempts to justify a higher margin in terms of credit worthiness go elsewhere! They are already charging a premium on business loans — for no apparent reason whatsoever.

As far as charges are concerned insist in writing that you'll be kept informed of all *extra* charges which will be levied. And query all charges not specified.

Ron, the owner-operator of a stationery retail/wholesale business in St Kilda, Melbourne, had a $100 000 business overdraft facility (secured by a registered debenture over the company assets). He did the sums to establish the true cost of his bank finance:

Upfront fees	$250
Ongoing fees	$700
Line fee	0.75%
Transaction fees (monthly average)	$35
Total cost (first year) (excluding interest)	$2120
Here, the base rate quoted was	10.25%
Base margin	2.5%
Above extras equate to	2.12%
Total (effective) rate	14.9%

And that was before any penalty rates were charged for over-the-limit transactions or any other application of penalty rates. (Note some banks have special penalty rate provisions which if triggered can add up to 8 percentage points to the base rate.)

When less is more

There are valuable lessons to be learned from Michael's challenge to the bank interest charges and Glen's and Iris's nightmare journey into a bank-financed business purchase. Too many small businesses fail because they are either under-capitalised or lumbering under too much debt. Each case provides us with basic commercial truth: watch the level of debt and watch the level of interest payments.

'I wanted to expand my retail hardware business by building a customer car-park in the rear. I didn't want to borrow all the money because the numbers just didn't stack up,' said Stan. 'The banks beat you all the time when you're in this position.

'In retail you really have to watch your pennies; margins are so tight these days. Any commercial loan costs thousands. I just couldn't justify borrowing from the bank and absorbing the costs.

'I had to completely re-assess how I was running the business. I tightened up my trade account ledger, offering discounts for cash settlements to my trade customers. I also spoke to my main suppliers of my plans, demonstrating the extra business that would be generated. I put to them the proposition that they extend their credit terms to 90 days while the project was being developed. They all accommodated me.

'Then I borrowed three lots of $7000 from family members, offering them 3 percentage points above bank deposit rates, feeling comfortable in the knowledge that I would repay them within twelve months and that $7000 would not be missed by them in the short term.'

These manoeuvres enabled Stan to raise $200 000 over the 90-day period of construction which, combined with a progressive and deferred payment schedule agreed with the builder, enabled him to amass the funds for his improvements.

No overdraft or bank borrowings were needed. But Stan did not stop here. Given his new-found zeal for beating the banks, Stan completely restructured his banking needs. 'I was running accounts like Topsy — just using them and opening up new ones whenever I needed a special-purpose account. Even petty cash had its own transaction account.

'I knew bank fees were eating up big dollops of cash and I knew I was losing interest by not putting surplus funds out onto the money market. What I did was go see my bank manager. But rather than go cap-in-hand, I went armed with a detailed cash flow statement and budgets, and demanded a better deal from him.

'What I got was a business transaction account that offered a combination of low fees based on my predicted usage, and high interest rates on any credit balances. Rather than pay me just over 3 per cent they agreed to pay me 6 per cent on credit balances over $25 000. I also negotiated a commercial acceptance facility at the most competitive rate.

'The bank originally asked for $2250 to cover establishment and loan service fees for a $200 000 facility. They quoted me a loan rate (base plus client margin) of 11.5 per cent. I pointed out that they were quoting their base (variable) rate at 9.15 per cent and that they were charging me a margin of more than 2 per cent. This was excessive given that mine was an established business with good security. We settled on $750 charges and a loan rate of 10.25 per cent; variable.'

By closing several accounts and renegotiating on credit balances, Stan calculated that during the first year alone he improved his cash flow by $4000.

'I asked for what I knew was right. I needed to feel in control again.' Stan repaid his family members six months later — with interest. He also worked out that the exercise saved him nearly $9000 in interest costs and bank charges for the loan that he didn't need.

'I work hard for my money. I don't want to see banks get more than their fair share,' he concluded.

Debt *can* enable your business to grow. And growth is the theme for most small to medium-sized businesses — even an upgrade can lead to growth. But the lessons from our stories suggest that a rethink of your business finances and your relationship with the banks need to come first.

Too many people lose their homes because they failed to see that bricks-and-mortar security is one way, but not the only way to secure bank finance.

How to select the right loan

What is available to small business today is a range of bank and non-bank products that offer much more flexibility for them. Credit unions and building societies are offering almost as many services as the banks.

And as with other forms of bank finance, business finance requires navigating through a maze of products. Westpac, for example, in its regular listing of lending rates for business loans, lists no less than nine rates! The Commonwealth Bank went even better — offering an extraordinary 13 different rates under their banner of *Commercial Loans*.

Apart from the obvious rule — don't borrow too much! — matching the business need with the type of loan is very important. A mismatch could mean thousands of dollars in unnecessary costs. Examine the needs of the business and match these to the lending facility. In the following pages, we'll look at the features that are important for your business loan.

Most businesses utilise one or more of the following types of bank loans:

- business transaction accounts and overdraft
- small business acceptance loans
- small business commercial loans
- lines of credit

- home equity-based business loans
- supplier credit.

Transaction accounts and overdraft

Ideally a business transaction account holds a combination of low fees, high interest rates on credit balances, a range of attached payment options, such as a cheque book and credit card, and an overdraft facility.

Overdrafts on transaction accounts have traditionally been the small business method of financing its day-to-day needs. A flexible loan linked to a cheque account which can be drawn on and repaid at any time provided the borrower remain within a predetermined set limit.

Such loans can, however, be costly. And since the fees and interest charged vary greatly from bank to bank, it is essential to know what the total costs — interest rate plus fees — are. Take care to check on the size of the line fee, which is charged simply for maintaining the overdraft facility (even if you don't use it).

While it is possible to get unsecured overdrafts you can expect the bank to require some from of security, the vast majority being bricks-and-mortar type. However, it is unlikely to be available should the outstanding amount of the current mortgage be valued at 80 per cent of the home or more.

Rates and fees vary widely between banks: from $32 to $43 monthly for fees, and $1100 to $3650 for the yearly fee charged on a $200 000 business overdraft facility. Overdraft base rates ranged from 10.2 per cent to 12.75 per cent, while typical *premiums* added ranged from 1.5 up to 3 per cent. (These accounts were assumed to run on an average number of transactions, including ATMs, other-the-counter withdrawals, cheque deposits, periodic payments, direct credits and up to 40 cheque withdrawals in a month.)

Apart from real estate, a business overdraft facility can often be secured by a registered debenture charge over company assets. Borrowers, provided they can demonstrate a successful track record for the business, should not have to pledge their house and home if they choose not to. Banks will almost always ask for this.

It is easy to see how crippling an indifferent approach to business banking could be with the possibility of an unfortunate business person penalised up to $10 000 in fees and charges if he or she was landed with the most expensive combination of costs.

But some good news is at hand, with banks starting to feel the heat of competition. Some banks now offer zero up-front fees and minimal ongoing fees, without the penalty of uncompetitive interest rates. Some non-banks, QIDC (Queensland Industry Development Corporation), for example, offer among the lowest interest rates and the lowest fee structures when compared with a range of banks. As we've already seen, the differences between low fees and excessive fees can be thousands of dollars.

Small business acceptance loans

In the case of a small business acceptance loan the borrower gives a written order to pay a specified amount of money at a future date. This written order or commercial bill is like a cheque drawn by a borrower to receive funds, but is not debited to the borrower's account until later. Meanwhile, the bill can be used immediately to raise finance.

Bank bills provide advantages to the small business person who knows how to gain financially from them. The potential for interest rate management and the impact on cash will be the deciding factors in choosing between a small business commercial loan and an acceptance facility.

Once you sign the bills, the bank buys them at a discount and credits you with the discounted amount less bank charges and stamp duty. On the due date, the face value of the bill must be repaid to the bank or you have to make other arrangements. The bill rate varies daily, reflecting money market activity. Once a rate is fixed to the bill, the rate is fixed until the due date.

Various fees apply to a bank bill facility. Usually you will pay an establishment fee and facility fee. Establishment fees may be scaled and vary between banks from 0.5 to 1.2 per cent. Other fees can include a handling fee, applied at the initial draw-down and at roll-overs of the bill, as well as stamp or loan duty.

Bank bill rates are quoted daily in the newspapers and those rates quoted have been used for the wholesale market. But take care, it can be misleading that you will also achieve the same rate reserved for larger blue chip borrowers.

Small business commercial loans

Loans on offer in this category were both of the variable and fixed variety. Typically, variable loans ranged between 9.7 per cent and 10.05 per cent, while fixed loans were from one to seven years, ranging from 9.15 to 10.05 per cent. These are all base rates to which a client margin may be added. A margin of 1.5 per cent would give an average rate of 10.45 (medium of quotes) per cent.

Incidentally, most banks assess *customer risk* based on a combination of the security offered: business history, character of the borrowers and cash flow. One bank commented that: 'We examine the cash flow first and then the security. Security might not be overly strong but the cash flow and history of the business might make it a viable proposition.'

Through increased competition between the banks and a knowledge of their products an informed borrower should be able to add a number of features to this facility such as being able to pay off the loan when they want, as well as having interest-only and principal and interest options. Also, rate and fee cutting should enable smart shopping to potentially prune 0.5 per cent from interest charges and more than $1000 from up-front fees.

Lines of credit

Commonly referred to as the 'come-and-go money', this form of finance can be used for working capital needs, cash flow arrangements or receivable financing. It offers advantages over other types of financing, because it is a loan that can be kept in reserve until you need it. You don't pay interest until you actually draw down on the facility.

Home equity-based business loans

With these types of loans most of the leading banks would offer a product which allows businesses to link their home loans with a business overdraft facility, giving them a common credit limit based on both loans.

The receipts from the business can be used to pay off the home loan while the business operations can be funded by dipping into the overdraft facility. The interest payments on the overdraft become tax deductable, allowing significant savings.

And as we saw in Chapter 8 an acceleration of the home loan can be very tax effective, given that surplus dollars will generate tax-free gains on the home.

Supplier credit

This is time given to pay a bill. It is an excellent facility for cash flow management — but beware of the hidden cost: some suppliers offer discounts for prompt payment. This can equate to a very high cost of finance if discount is foregone.

You might also check out those institutions that offer *special loan programs* to help firms like yours finance start-up costs and expansion plans. And remember to look for alternatives to debt for those expansion plans. Take note of Stan's strategy for avoiding too much debt.

Also consider outside equity; that is, partners. If you look around, you may find someone who has gone this route. Check it out — there are many avenues available for bringing in outside capital — and remember you don't have to relinquish control.

Bricks and mortar

No risk finance! — from the bank's point of view. From the stories I've heard, many of which can indeed be called horror stories, there is one disturbing theme that tears through my mind: the banks' absolute need for bricks-and-mortar security is more often than not the starting point, often leading to loans being granted where the business's case was not strong enough. Banks tend to look for real estate as security but there are other options.

In the case of small business loans it doesn't make sense to lodge security worth hundreds of thousands of dollars to support loans as little as \$10 000. Should you default, the bank would sell up the home. If you are starting a business from scratch it may not be possible to avoid putting up your house as security. But if the business has been trading for a while it should have assets of some kind and a cash flow.

Assets can be pledged, and lending against receivables is becoming acceptable, although proof will have to be established that orders will translate into a reliable cash flow.

Some banks will offer mortgage-free overdrafts without providing direct security. Westpac, for example, provides up to \$20 000 in its product. For company borrowers all that they require is a director's guarantee. The product is available to approved borrowers who have a strong credit history and total borrowings reliant on the business cash flow of less than $250 000. Westpac advises that you should also have net assets (not for security purposes) of at least $75 000 and own an interest in either residential or commercial real estate.

You will need to have resolve to stand up to the banks when they demand bricks-and-mortar security. You need to prepare a good business case for presenting the potential security value of each element of the business.

Negotiate from a position of knowledge of what represents a good business risk from the bank's point of view. The key is to negotiate rather than be intimidated by the bank's request for the home as security. Lenders today have become far more flexible and if you find your bank inflexible, consider moving on.

How to get a better deal from the bank

The following tips have been designed to help you get a better deal:

Determine your needs. Get a handle on what your business's average daily balance might be and how often you'll need to make transactions; for example, deposits and cheques.

Define your banking style. If you believe that low fees are important to your business you might consider establishing a relationship with a local credit union. Generally, the fees charged by commercial banks are higher than those at credit unions, but there's a trade-off: commercial banks offer business loans, whereas most credit unions don't.

So, if you're in the market for a small business loan try a

niche banker that specialises in such financing. Each state has its niche institutions; for example, St George in NSW, Bank of Melbourne in Victoria, Challenge in WA and QIDC in Queensland.

Check out the location. You don't want to burden yourself with a 30-minute drive every other week to do your commercial banking, although it should not be your main consideration for going with one bank over another. Good service and reasonable rates should be.

Research fees. With minimum fees ranging from $30 to $40 monthly for a business account, in addition to the fees already being paid on personal accounts, business owners can't afford not to research bank fees and minimum balances. Because bank services and fees for business banking vary widely it is best to choose three banks (including your current one) to compare their fees and services.

Negotiate. If you don't ask, you'll never know whether a bank is willing to negotiate any of its fees or services, so go ahead and inquire. Some of the more popular concessions financial institutions make tend to be fee waivers, free cheques, ATM cards, and numerous others. But go in armed with information about your bank's indicator base rate for commercial loans and details of securities such as assets and debtors.

There is little doubt that if you have been in business for two years or more, and have a good credit history, you should be able to get a better deal from your bank than you are getting at the moment.

The future is here

The future may indeed have arrived for small business as far as banking is concerned — if it can go on-line. This can provide some genuine money-saving opportunities. Consider the following:

Bank accounts readable from an office computer have been progressively launched by a number of the banks over the past 12 months as part of a growing move to electronic banking to meet the needs of small business.

Using standard computers and software a business can tap into bank branches locally and internationally (where available) to read account balances, make payments and transfer funds. This is a natural extension of what is already available to businesses and if software is not already in the workplace, very reasonably priced packages are available.

With electronic banking the customer can import a bank statement directly into accounting software, avoid re-keying, and know the full extent of the business's financial position quickly.

A key attraction for services currently available from a number of the larger banks (e.g. Commonwealth, ANZ and National) is that customers can pay both their staff and suppliers electronically, cutting out the need for a cheque book. Not only does this minimise debits taxes by making multiple transactions in one move, but it cuts mailing time and costs.

And most critically, it allows for exact cash flow management, given there is no uncertainty as to when cheques drawn on the business account are presented to the bank.

Plastic banking

The Commonwealth Bank, for example, has introduced a credit card that small business can use in conjunction with a line of credit of up to $100 000. Once again this facility provides simplified, cost-effective banking.

The card is designed to meet the cash flow needs of the small trader and the small business owner. The service is available on an unsecured as well as a secured basis to any credit-worthy business that has been in operation for more than two years. In an attempt to pre-empt fears about add-on charges, the bank has struck an *all up* interest rate of 14 per cent a year, which is inclusive of account-keeping charges.

In keeping up with consumers' desire to have flexibility around banking hours — no more queues — card accounts may be paid via ATM or Eftpos. In effect the card is a line of credit, and interest is charged only on the outstanding balance; that is, without client margins. For small traders, especially those who have tended to mix their own personal transactions and plastic with business, this service separates the two and also draws a business into business finance, thus allowing the trader to build a credit profile.

This is great idea for those who want to reduce account-keeping fees for over-used transaction accounts!

Tip-offs to rip-offs

- Check your bank's charges for electronic banking.
- Check its security arrangements. Look for the latest in encryption technology.
- Ask for the accounting software!

Check list for business banking

- Review all bank accounts. Can they be linked and merged?
- Review all bank loans. How much are they actually costing? How much over the bank's base rate are you

being charged? (Include charges relating to any mortgage facility which may support a business loan.)

- How much do you pay in bank fees each year? (A small business such as Stan's would incur fees of up to $30–$40 per month for each account, assuming, for example, 40 cheque withdrawals).
- How accurately do you monitor cash flow?
- Do you have an accurate picture of debtors and creditors?
- Can you use supplier credit more effectively?
- When was the last time negotiated with the bank?
- Prepare a cash flow statement and budgets for presentation to your bank. Ask your accountant to assist.
- Make sure you *always* receive copies of *every* document signed. And don't sign anything you don't completely understand.

Chapter 13
Bank discrimination

'I'm still trying to pick myself up off the floor.' Jane had applied for a business loan from her local bank. She'd been running a physiotherapy practice in Sydney's Redfern district for a year or so now, and was looking to set up a better equipped operation. She needed $25 000. She had a small mortgage on her semi in Bondi and had few other debts. Her application was refused.

'The bank sent a commercial lending person to my home. The young man in his late 20s was very business-like. The interview went something like this:

'"How old are you Ms Pettorino?"

'"51."

'"Are you currently married?"

'"No. Divorced."

'"Do you have children living with you?"

'"No. What relevance is all this? I thought we were looking at a business loan, not a dating service."

'"Just completing the application, Ms Pettorino."

'"It's Mrs Pettorino."

'"Sorry, Mrs. Now I need to ask about your income history. When did you rejoin the workforce?"

'"I only left the workforce for a short time. But that was many years ago. Surely the only thing that matters is my ability to service the loan?"

'"Yes, that's what I'm looking at now," said the young bank man.'

As women are increasing their economic power, banks are now trying to redress the imbalances of the past. So much has the situation changed that the banks are desperately positioning themselves to catch up to today's reality. Women are potent competitors in the income stakes.

In many cases women are now out-stripping their husbands financially. A recent article in *Psychology Today* says we can no longer sweep female power under the cultural rug. 'Seven million American women earned more than their mates in 1993 and last year almost a quarter of all working wives out-earned their husbands.'

Banks, ever reluctant to admit past mistakes, are now aggressively presenting a new face. Banks can't afford to discriminate towards staff or customers. A spokesperson from the National Australia Bank, for example, did admit that: 'Women are not having children until later and they are staying in the workforce longer.' And while this may not be news to women it does suggest a degree of willingness to cast off old shackles in attitudes in banking institutions.

But one of the more substantive ways in which banks are addressing the issue is by putting more female staff into senior positions. They are now increasingly promoting females up the ranks — appointing them to managerial positions and turning them into bank managers in a desperate bid to gain a chunk of the lucrative female market.

Westpac, for instance, has appointed hundreds of female managers in recent years. The culture has had to change dramatically in order for this to happen. Formerly managers had to move up the ranks from teller to accountant and up the slippery ladder. Women didn't ever get past a certain point due not just to prejudice but also because many left to start families in a time when childcare wasn't a consideration.

One female manager says that what she experienced is more a case of 'ageism' than sexism internally because 'she hasn't paid her dues but the old guard tolerate it'. In order to rectify the imbalance of females in senior management many younger women have had to be catapulted up the ranks without paying their dues. This has been part of the shake-up internally in the banking system. And it's caused much internal resentment and friction. However, it is a cost worth paying.

Newcomers — male or female — are often regarded with a degree of suspicion by the *old guard.* Like the desperate attempts to win back customer support after the debacles of the early 1990s, this is catch up stuff.

'It is not just to lure women customers. They've done studies which have shown that women are better at selling and handling people across the board. They're much more customer service oriented.' Jane is one of the new breed of female bank managers. 'But it's particularly good for women customers. I've heard many horror stories about women being asked their age. One very professional woman was recently turned down because they told her she was of child-bearing age — in the 1990s!! Another two women I know who are in business together told me they were made to feel very uncomfortable by an intimidating older man in a business suit.

'That's the thing about me. I have a different way of operating. I look only at the numbers. Not the sex of the applicant.

Not how you are dressed. You can come in dressed informally, have a coffee and a chat. I'm not looking at all that superficial stuff. When I came to this job I insisted on a round table so I could be closer to the customers and make them feel more comfortable at all levels.

'I think discrimination against women clients is definitely a thing of the past but it's been a long battle. Even as a female manager I was asked up until recently if I was the manager's secretary.'

Another senior manager in a large bank says: 'The culture for women has changed both as clients and management. In an aggressive market battle for the customer, the whole way of viewing women has had to change in order not to miss out on valuable clients; on the female dollar. I don't think women should put up with sexism any more.'

Not all women complain of sexism. One talked of being treated respectfully even though she expressed a desire to have children in the foreseeable future. 'They were looking more at my wallet than my legs,' she recalled. 'I was very impressed with their attitude. The manager was a male but very informal and relaxed.'

However another woman applying for a home loan with her husband was treated in a not-so-subtle sexist manner by a male manager, who once again raised the stale bogey of 'are you planning a family' as if to remind them of the possible financial *risk* attached to this. So it still depends on *which bank*.

Financial planning

Attitudes on the part of the banks are one thing but there is still the reality that sound financial planning for women requires special consideration. Although women are delaying having children and returning to the workforce sooner, there's little doubt that plans need to be made.

Cassie, a career journalist, waited until she was 34 before having her first child. She was in a relationship but wished to retain her financial independence.

'It was very important for me. I desperately wanted to have a child but I love my career and I visualised returning to work as soon as practicable.

'But I'd taken on a huge financial commitment in the form of a mortgage and the repayments needed to be met. I needed $100 000 for my property purchase so I borrowed $110 000. That way I put $10 000 in a high-yield account and that allowed me to service my mortgage repayments while I stopped work. OK there was some interest to pay, but I was in total control. No stress.'

Some banks will offer flexibility in terms of reduced payments for parental leave purposes. Westpac, for example, in its premium option loan offers this facility for up to six months.

Financial planning does not concern just women planning to have children. Married women have particular challenges. Adopting *his* surname for the purposes of banking and finance may be convenient, but it raises some thorny issues, not the least of which concerns a married woman's own credit *rating*. As already noted in Chapter 10, keep your own credit card, if for no other reason than to establish that you have not acted in a manner not worthy of credit.

Mary was now alone. Although she had her own home as a result of her divorce, she now needed to build her own identity as a single person, not just the Mrs in Mr and Mrs. She'd already encountered her first challenge: she was refused a credit card by her bank.

'Twelve years as a married woman left me without an identity. It would've been much easier if I'd have kept my credit card from my singles days.

'I really want to go back to my birth name.'

A number of commentators have observed that women were far less likely to have planned for retirement, for example, than men. Associate Professor Jenny Onyx, of the University of Technology in Sydney, in a study based on 800 interviews confirmed this. Professor Onyx said that a large percentage of women — up to 50 per cent — received no information about retirement. 'This compared with 26 per cent of men who had said they had received no information about retirement.'

Professor Onyx also found that women contributed to funds at a lower rate than men. She attributed a lack of planning and awareness to the fact that many married women expected to be able to draw on a spouse's superannuation or on a government pension.

Financial institutions, particularly banks, have lagged in redressing this issue, leaving women generally with no information or in seeking other networks from which to draw advice.

Seniors: the unkindest cut of all

There is no reluctance when it comes to tagging our senior citizens as a bank disadvantaged group.

This group, according to Gerard Thomas, policy officer of the Pensioners' and Superannuants' Federation, suffers an institutional form of financial abuse.

Gerard was speaking of the banks and how their treatment of senior citizens as a group was viewed by many in the community. He was also speaking of the problem that many senior citizens have in managing their money.

'We have serious concerns that we have asked the banks to address. We are concerned about the pace of change and how this translates into branches being replaced by kiosk-style banking and ATMs. Many elderly people need the branch network.'

It is typical for a senior citizen to see the changes in banking as follows: 'A lot of us are nervous about withdrawing money in the street. You worry someone will whizz up, grab your bag and run off. That's why I use my cheque account and telephone to pay all my bills.'

Thomas added: 'These are people who have been used to seeing the same manager in the branch over many years, and who were loyal to the bank from the day they put their first shilling into their passbooks. Often our members have difficulty with some of the new banking trends such as Eftpos and, for example, knowing the difference between charge and credit cards.

'The elderly are disadvantaged when it comes to service. They are often the first to suffer but the last to complain.' Thomas notes that in terms of being informed, senior citizens are not in a strong position. They're the least informed when it comes to access for redress. And they are among the least well represented when it comes to complaint handling via the Banking Ombudsman for example.

The Ombudsman's annual report reveals that the scheme is over-represented in the 35 to 65 age group, suggesting that the elderly are not significant complainants.

Gerard Thomas expresses some concern about the pace of change and the effect of inevitable mergers. 'I have some sympathy for the banks who need to rationalise the branch network to contain costs, but what we are seeking is an accommodation of our members' concerns and needs.'

The Pensioners' and Superanuants' Federation has lobbied government and the banks for better deals for retirees and pensioners. However, Thomas believes that banks see senior citizens as a *win-win* situation. 'What they've got are very large balances in relatively low cost accounts. Retirees as a group have $25 billion invested in bank and other deposits.'

In a typical two-week period, the Department of Social

Security will pay more than $1.2 billion into the accounts of Australian pensioners and beneficiaries. Some of these deposits will be available to the banks for the short-term money market.

It is even more incredible that banks offer little in the way of special consideration for this group — they are a cash cow for the banks with large passive deposits in often low interest-bearing accounts

What is more disturbing is the way banks use their combined might. Banks, ever keen to protect their profits, recently put forward plans to cut rates on the special accounts for pensioners known as *deeming accounts*.* The banks lobbied aggressively for the top rate paid on deeming accounts to be cut from 7 to 5.5 per cent — even though rates set by the Reserve Bank had fallen only 1 per cent since July. In a compromise move announced late last year, the deeming rates have been reduced to a maximum 6 per cent.

That may be great for the banks but once again not so hot for pensioners. Many retirees, now only in their late 60s, retired when interest rates were in the mid teens. This means that on a lump sum of $200 000 they earned an income of $30 000. Today, interest rates are less than half, slashing many retirees' incomes by the same proportion.

For many retirees the first and only stop is the bank. Armed with their termination payments, superannuation funds, etc, many invest in the banks' subsidiary products — approved deposit funds, deferred annuities, and so on — in the belief that the bank guarantees these products. Often in the small print lies

* Deeming accounts are special accounts, available only to older people and/or social security recipients. They were introduced in 1992 to encourage pensioners to seek a better return on their savings. Under the government's deeming policy, a pensioner's cash or savings (above $2000 each) are assessed for tax and other purposes as if they are earning interest at a set rate (currently the deeming rates are set at 5 per cent and 7 per cent). These rates are reviewed regularly and may be varied both up and down.

the truth: 'The bank does not guarantee the performance of the fund or the repayment of capital.'

While banks remain the preferred place for retirees and the elderly to seek information, it is the independently funded National Information Centre on Retirement Investments that provides much of the information that retirees and the elderly can use as a basis for independent decision making.

Wendy Shield, an executive with the group, believes there is a huge pool of uninformed people out there when it comes to knowing how to best protect their savings. 'The elderly are particularly vulnerable because they don't have the financial literacy of many younger people. As a consequence they get ripped off.'

Trusting the bank?

According to Gerard Thomas there is a degree of mistrust emerging on the part of many elderly when it comes to advice. Based on my own anecdotal evidence the cynicism is even more widespread than that with people genuinely fed up with huge bank profits and falling personal savings. All the legacy of the huge decline in interest rates over the past five years combined with a massive rebuilding of bank profits. Against this is the backdrop of declining bank branches, increased emphasis toward electronic banking and, in some cases, the complete scrapping by banks of the ordinary pass-book account.

Few banks are going against this trend, but there is one notable exception: Westpac, which has launched special retiree products. As long as retirees and the elderly require the security of knowledge that their funds are safe in bank accounts, they are at risk of having funds tied up in non-performing assets.

According to the Australian Pensioners' and Superannuants' Federation, while older people can and do look out for a better rate of interest they find the means of calculating it quite baffling and in many cases deceitful. This is particularly the case with the payment of stepped and tiered interest rates, with only three out of 80 people in focus group research recognising the impact that the different rates of interest have on overall returns on their savings.

There is an onus of responsibility on the part of banks to act in a socially responsible manner. There is also a lot of anxiety because those who have stuck with their preferred investment options of term deposits have seen their incomes dwindle. Older investors have a strong preference for liquid, low risk investments. Because of their age they worry about locking money away. They like to hold cash and invest in fixed rates for a year or less.

It is difficult to blame the banks alone for the plight of retirees dependent on fixed income. The need for security and the association of this with banks is a long-standing tradition. Unfortunately, the answer in terms of protecting capital and ensuring a proper *living* income comes with a diversification *away* from cash and bank deposits.

Chapter 14

Laughing all the way to the bank: the ultimate revenge

James hated banks with a passion. He couldn't understand why anyone would want to deal with them. 'They're only there to make their shareholders wealthy. They're robber barons'.

While James may have been mad, these are not the views of a madman. James is a senior manger of a large Melbourne-based department store. 'I keep a no-fee transaction account at the bank for bills I can't pay by cash or by phone. But as far as the rest is concerned. No way. They will not get my money.

'I don't know how much they've cost me over the years. Tens of thousands of dollars, I guess.'

The tens of thousands James is referring to is the sum total not only of fees and bank charges, but also of lost opportunities. Because, like most people, James had believed that a savings account at the bank was necessary, secure and accessible.

James, with his home paid off, has more flexibility and options as far as his income is concerned. 'What you find when you've reached middle age and your home is just about paid for is that you begin to focus on the investment side of the equation. You no longer take for granted that banks are there to protect you. They're not. You see, inflation is the real enemy of your savings. And money in the bank has no protection against it. There's no safety net. I never got any help from the bank ever.

'My accountant pointed out a couple of years ago that even higher interest rates on deposits aren't the answer. He told me about franked dividends on shares. He also told me that bonds can pay far higher returns than bank term deposits.

'I learned that some companies pay dividends that are effectively tax free in your hands. Not surprisingly, some of the best dividend paying stocks are the banks.

'My accountant showed me some figures and what they revealed was that over a long term, income — in the form of dividends — has been paid at about the same rate as interest on term deposits. This income is virtually tax free in my hands.* Also this income tends to grow every year as dividends grow. And I don't have to worry about whether share markets go up or down because I don't intend selling them.'

Advice is there for the asking — accountants, friends, professional advisers — just don't ask the bank!

James is a tax hero. He has invested his money in such a way as to minimise his tax and at the same time preserve and even grow his capital. Although James is not a corporate high flier, he has managed to beat the system and profit from it by doing some homework, seeking the best advise he could find — and by taking his money out of the bank.

*Fully franked dividends — 36 per cent tax paid — produce little or no additional income tax liability for the average investor.

Once a fortress, the banking sector is falling under increasing attack. An upturn in financially literate consumers means banks no longer have the monopoly of our money business. Alternative mortgage lenders, armed with laptop computers, are storming the market and taking home loan opportunities from the banks.

And the bank manager, once the person to approach with financial queries, is being replaced by software financial planning packages and telephone inquiry centres. So where do we put our hard-earned dollars? And who do we trust for advice?

Remember, we're not just talking about trust here; we're talking about *smart* and all the *smart* money I have ever seen does not put investment money in the bank. At least not for the long term.

In an ideal world most people would want two types of accounts for their surplus funds: a *rainy day* or cash account and a savings/investment account. Tying up all your money in a long-term investment would be unwise if you are going to need money in an emergency.

Let's look at where funds can be kept that take into account the need to keep funds at hand and balance this with the fundamental need to preserve your capital.

Term deposits

Term deposits are interest-bearing accounts offered by banks, building societies and credit unions. The interest rate is fixed for a selected period of time, generally ranging from seven days to five years. Penalties for withdrawal before maturity may apply. However, 'Term deposits are not long-term investments'. Rothschild Australia hammered this point in a series of ads promoting the concept of managed funds. Rothschild, an international firm of investment bankers and fund managers, claimed that term deposits delivered a much lower return than managed investments in shares, for example.

Over the long term, when you take tax and inflation into consideration, term deposits do not stack up very well against managed investments. Investment returns for *cash* (bank accounts and money market investments) averaged 7.4 per cent over the five years to the end of 1995. Over the same period Australian shares averaged a return of 15.9 per cent. When taxes are factored in, the gap widens even more as some dividends received on shares are effectively tax free in the hands of many investors.

Because of their security, fixed term deposits are very popular in Australia. However, if you are considering regularly rolling over term deposits as a longer term strategy it could mean you are missing out on the potential for real investment growth and even basic capital preservation. Further, early withdrawal of your money from most term deposits can come at a cost, which usually means your investment actually achieves a much lower rate of return than expected.

With the massive decline in interest rates experienced over the past five years the tendency for retirees, in particular, to lock their money away in term deposits at banks and live off the interest has been seriously challenged. The idea was that while there was a *nest egg* there would always be an income stream, but concurrent low interest rates and low inflation have put an end to that.

What is disturbing is the degree to which many retirees and the elderly do not always have information as to how they can increase returns on their funds while keeping within their tax and benefits thresholds. And banks with their captive client base have not been the ones to tell retirees that term deposits alone, particularly bank term deposits, are *not* the *safe* way to go.

Cash management trusts

As bank deposit rates slide into oblivion, investors and savers (is there a difference?) are turning to cash management trusts in a search for performance. In one 12-week period last year, cash management trusts received a net inflow of funds totalling nearly $2 billion, most of it coming from the bank coffers of depositors, switching funds to get a better return.

Smart money moving in the one direction is certainly something for all savers and investors to take note of. Smart money beats the banks and profits from it.

Cash management trusts are unit trusts which allow investors to pool their money in the short-term money market. The security and access to money invested in cash management trusts is outlined in the prospectus. Cash management trusts that invest only in government or bank-backed investments are low risk.

There are roughly 100 cash management trusts operating by both bank and non-bank enterprises such as building societies, credit unions and insurance companies. It is certainly worth shopping around, not only for a decent interest rate but also for the sort of account which is tailored to suit your lifestyle (e.g. minimum deposit and location).

Cash trusts offer a better return on the readily available accounts for those with less than $50 000 to invest. Cash trusts have since inception traditionally paid the same rate irrespective of the amount invested. The banks, on the other hand, have always discriminated against the smaller investor, tending to offer much higher rates for the larger amounts.

The differences between the rates paid by cash trusts and bank cash management accounts can be substantial, particularly for the smaller amounts.

On an amount of $6000, for example, the ANZ was paying less than 3 per cent while Macquarie cash management trust was paying 5.7 per cent at the time of writing. Some trusts paid in excess of 6 per cent at the time for amounts as little as $1000. In order to achieve a similar return from a bank an investor would need to tie up $50 000 for 6 months! The cash trusts, on the other hand, can offer same-day withdrawal facilities with no penalty.

While some cash trusts also provide a cheque facility and electronic access, the main disadvantage of cash trusts is that they are not all accessible via a branch network. This presents some inconvenience when a new cheque book is needed or in the case of the need for a bank cheque. Also cash deposits and withdrawals are usually not possible. In most cases this will require a visit to the bank after a transfer.

The other disadvantage is that cash trust rates are linked directly to money market rates; this means that rates on offer are changing all the time. Generally the movements are small. And this can be an advantage when rates are rising as banks are very slow to pass on rate increases.

Cash trusts offer something the banks do not offer: a high return. For those who are willing to use electronic means to move funds around from their bank transaction account, cash trusts offer convenience and no more bank queues!

Fixed interest securities

These encompass any investment which has an interest rate attached to it and which guarantees the return of capital. This includes everything from the humble savings account, term deposits and cash management trusts, to negotiable securities. Some common fixed interest investments which are negotiable are debentures (usually offered by finance companies), unsecured notes (usually offered as an alternative to debentures by smaller companies) and bonds.

Negotiable securities offer an opportunity to squeeze

higher returns out of fixed interest securities without significant risks. According to Tony Lewis, managing director of Lewis Securities, a broking house specialising in fixed interest securities, 'tradeable fixed-interest securities are much better than straight term deposits at the bank because they give flexibility back to the investor'.

Debentures, government bonds and utilities can offer investors higher yields than both bank deposits and cash management trusts with little or no increased risk. They can be bought and sold on the market through a stockbroker, thus offering investors ready liquidity. Once again, the plan is designed to compliment an investment strategy rather than being a total solution in itself.

Many retirees are now realising that good times — like the period 1990–91 when interest rates were high — come and go, and that other options, such as shares or debentures, need to be looked at.

With complex deeming rules and sophisticated products such as allocated pensions and annuities, retirees, in particular, are required to become better informed, even before turning to professional advisers.

Longer term investments

Richard Duncan took his first plunge into stocks 10 years ago when share markets around the world were booming. It took $10 000 for Richard to see the danger of poor investment advice, or more to the point, word-of-mouth stock tips.

Australian entrepreneurs were going to take over the world. Investing in the likes of Alan Bond, Christopher Skase and John Elliott was going to double, then quadruple your money within a few years.

This was the advice of a *professional* adviser. For all it was worth it could have been the advice of a young bell-hop at any hotel. Richard lost all his money, but it taught him three valuable lessons:

- Timing. People always want to join in the fun when markets — both share and property — are rising. What it really needs is a more disciplined approach.
- Homework. Successful investors do very serious research.
- 'Don't put all your eggs in the one basket'.

Investing your money shouldn't involve huge investments of time, yet working out how to get the best return from your money can be a full-time job. This is not a job for the faint-hearted. Look at what happened when we sought the advice of a panel of advisers:

Question: Where would you invest $25,000?

Adviser 1:
'I'd top up my compulsory superannuation — you only pay 15 per cent tax.' But the big drawback here is that you can't get your hands on your money until you're
55 and retired!

Adviser 2:
'My money would go into a mix of trusts; both equity and property — offering a mixture of income and growth. I believe the bank's performance in managing funds such as this is excellent.'

Adviser 3:
'I'd put the funds into a mix of fixed interest and managed funds. I'd buy a couple of utility-type bonds on the secondary market; leave some in a cash management trust and the rest in

two managed equity funds. One for dividend imputation the other in an international equity trust to take advantage of superior opportunities on overseas sharemarkets.'

Adviser 4:
'I'd open an account with an equity fund; split between high growth and yield. I'd add $100 a month from my salary to help grow the fund.'

Confused or bemused? These answers demonstrate the conflicting advice. What you *should* feel is a healthy dose of fear. Fear that you make the right choice of investment adviser! In the following pages, we'll take a look at some ground rules in selecting the right investment adviser for you.

Be prepared to understand and, if necessary, speak the jargon. If you're going to use professional fund managers, for example, (they may already be managing your super fund) then questions need to be asked. What style of manager? Is your manager a top-down, bottom-up, value, growth, thematic or a business-cycle manager?

If the jargon is too troublesome then professional advice may be the answer.

Advice from the bank: don't bank on it!

Mrs E, 69, held a $100 000 fixed term interest-bearing deposit which she had renewed annually for a number of years. On this occasion she was referred to a financial adviser with the bank, who told her he would help her invest the money. The majority of the funds were invested in two unit trusts administered by the bank.

After 12 months Mrs E returned to the bank to reinvest her savings which she believed were soon to fall due. She was dismayed to learn that the $80 000 invested in these trusts had a redemption value of $70 000. Mrs E said she believed the funds were reinvested on a similar basis to that in the past and said she had no understanding of the documentation she had signed.

This case was reported to the Australian Banking Industry Ombudsman (ABIO).The bank provided documentation from the interview supporting its position that Mrs E had been provided with sufficient information to make her decision an informed one, that the investments recommended were appropriate for her, and that they met her requirements at the time.

The ABIO suggested that the capital investment be restored by the bank as the income projections did not demonstrate higher returns than term deposits at the rates available at the relevant time, and that an investment of at least three years was necessary simply to recoup the up-front fees.

The ABIO case manager's opinion was that given Mrs E's history of simple investment products, she was not equipped to assess the nature of the risk inherent in the investment, and that managed funds were not an appropriate investment for her. The bank agreed to this suggested settlement and reinstated Mrs E's capital investment.

Here, bank customers are ripe for the picking, with the elderly and retirees being particularly vulnerable. Many bank branches today have an investment adviser available at the branch for consultation.

I tried one out and found, not surprisingly that what I was being shown was a series of brochures offering various bank managed investments, both share trusts and property trusts. I inquired whether these products were, first, suitable for my particular needs, and second, how this bank had performed compared with other comparable bank and non-bank products.

Although I was shown a table of comparison with other

unit trusts it was clear that the table was inadequate and did not answer the question. As far as my particular needs were concerned, the adviser suggested that a more detailed analysis would be required and that another appointment would need to be made. At least he was right on that score!

It would have to be an area of questionable competence on the part of banks to pose as investment advisers. Investment advising is a very complex business, with the area of superannuation alone an absolute minefield. New managed products appear every day, and to have a bank offering *independent* investment advice with its own interest to promote its own products must surely rank as one of the greatest examples of potential conflict of interest ever seen. It is simply pushing reality to suggest that the best advice is forthcoming while still offering bank-owned managed funds.

The *official* word on bank advice (quoted from the ABIO's 1995 annual report) is that: 'Bank staff are restricted generally from being able to provide advice about investment products. The bank's obligations usually extend only to accurately presenting the choices available. Consumers who feel they need assistance to select the most suitable investment vehicle should be referred to a licensed investment adviser.'

Banks as investment managers

Considering the issue of incompetence, I have looked at the performance tables and have consulted a leading firm of actuarial consultants — Mercer and Co. — who are experts in the field of comparing the performance of one investment manager against another. In, for example, the area of equities (pooled fund survey for the year ending September 1996) banks, as investment managers, do not even appear in the top ten.

Moreover, several very large banks reported such low investment returns in a number of investment products that investors would have been better off leaving their money in the bank — and in the lowest earning accounts for that matter!

Banks promoting their own savings accounts are one thing but banks promoting their investment products to a very large and often uninformed captive market needs to be watched very closely. At the very least an independent assessment of any product should be conducted before any money changes hands.

Bank advice may be very limited in its value, but most people don't see themselves seeking independent advice. Any anxiety aside many people do seek advice from professionals such as accountants. In fact, according to a survey late last year, accountants are the most popular source of investment advice for Australians.

Meanwhile what makes a good adviser?

Here the Australian Securities Commission (ASC) says a planner/adviser must be aware of the many different investment products in the marketplace, the risks and returns of those products, and how appropriate they are for the client's financial position and objectives. The planner must have appropriate training, qualifications and experience, and belong to governing bodies such as the Financial Planning Association.

Where do you find a financial adviser?

In the Yellow Pages, of course, under *financial planning*. Check several out and make sure they're licensed. They should hold the proper authority under the Corporations Code. Better still, ask your more successful friends who they might recommend as an independent adviser.

Checklist for those choosing an investment adviser or financial planner:

- Do your homework first. You need to have a basic knowledge of investment.
- Contact the Financial Planning Association (FPA) and ask them for guidance on adviser selection. It is a reputable body, with its members properly licensed by the ASC. The FPA has established a free Complaints Resolution Scheme. This means that if you have a genuine complaint about negligent or inappropriate advice received from a financial planner whose company is a member of the FPA, the matter will be investigated.
- Don't rely on bank advisers except as a preliminary step in your homework.
- Go to a firm with a reasonably long track record of operations and check the ownership. If it is owned by an insurance company or bank, there is a real risk that they will tend to flog those products generated by the parent company.
- Ask what research is done by the adviser to support any recommendations made.
- Check what ongoing services are provided by the adviser/firm and what the charges are.
- Check how the adviser gets paid. They can be paid in a number of ways:
  - By charging fees for work done, such as producing a written financial plan.
  - By receiving a commission (or brokerage) from an entry fee you pay to the investment institution.
  - By charging a scale of fees based on the total funds you invest.
  - By being paid by a combination of fees and commission.

Tip: You should with most reputable firms be able to get a free initial consultation.

Can ordinary people benefit from investment advice?

While financial advice and planning has an image as a service mainly for retirees and older people it is probably the case that younger people need advice even more. The problem is, as with older people, many just don't know where to start.

Now, when Annette, aged 25, browses through the racks of CDs and outfits on sale, she thinks about investment portfolios. The investment adviser she visited the previous month had an extraordinary effect on her.

Annette has taken her first steps to financial independence. She has put $1000 of her bank savings to work by investing in a managed equity fund. She has also committed to investing $200 each month into purchasing more units in the fund. This she has done by simply arranging for a periodic payment to be made out of her transaction account at her bank to the fund manager's account.

'It's a really good feeling knowing that I've taken control. No longer are savings something left to chance. And with only modest growth I know I'll probably have enough to put a decent deposit on a property before my thirtieth birthday.

'People spend their money first and what's left over they consider saving. In today's lifestyle there's nothing left over.'

I think we all relate to that! What the investment advice route makes available to the *younger population*, is the opportunity to turn this lifestyle on its head.

One investment adviser I spoke to summed it all up by asking: 'Will $25 a week disrupt you from enjoying the lifestyle you want? You don't get anything without sacrifice. You don't achieve goals without some form of discipline.'

Yes, there can be benefits from early counselling from an adviser:

- They can help you establish goals and set a plan for achieving them.
- They can assist you in the identification of any financial problems and help focus on good money management.

Shares: beating the banks

It's every investors' dream: high returns, no risk. Smart investors have long known that it is far smarter to invest in banks than it is to deposit your money with them.

I was shocked when I saw the figures: the banks as a group increased a massive 42 per cent (J. B. Were, *Australian Financial Review,* 21 October 1996) in value in one year alone to 30 September 1996. Extraordinary returns in anyone's language.

Given our case that banks are in the business of maximising shareholder wealth, it is not surprising to find that buying bank shares has been a much smarter strategy than putting your money in the bank. The trouble is, of course, that unlike bank deposits, your return on shares isn't guaranteed. And unlike bank deposits, the value can fluctuate daily, and for all practical purposes cannot be got at immediately. For many, this sort of uncertainty would be reason enough to do nothing. But doing nothing — in other words leaving money in the bank — may be the very worst thing to do. In this section we'll look at shares as an alternative; this is not advice, but merely a weighing up of the investment possibilities.

For most of us the concept of tax-free dividend income sounds a bit rich and left for those with high-priced accountants and advisers While interest income is taxed at the marginal tax rate, in many cases dividend income is tax fee. Cash deposits or even government bonds are not. If you receive $1000 in dividends from shares the chances are the company has already met up to 36 per cent of your tax responsibility. The tax office takes into account the tax already paid, substantially reducing the tax payable by you as an individual tax payer — this is known as dividend imputation, franked dividends or franking credits. If your personal tax rate is less than 36 per cent you will be able to claim the difference as a tax credit against other sources of income.

What people should realise is that although the price of shares can vary the income from the shares can be quite stable. People shouldn't, if retired for example, have too much trouble finding a regular source of income through a share portfolio forming part of an overall investment portfolio.

Baby boomers now between their late thirties and early fifties don't share their parent's views that shares are far too risky for small investors and that true long-term savings should be locked up in a bank account. It would appear, on balance, that one *can* take a plunge without too much fear or trepidation into share ownership. And there is the possibility of shareholder privileges as well.

Shareholder privilege

Owners of Coles Myer shares get them. Owners of Harvey Norman shares get them. And now owners of ANZ and NAB also get them. The *them* is shareholder privileges. Owners of these company shares and others are entitled to receive benefits, as shareholders, by shopping at or using the services of the companies they have invested in. Thus, not only do they participate in the profits of the company by way of receiving dividends and possibly long-term capital gains, but they can receive discounts or other entitlements by claiming share ownership. In the case of Coles Myer it is simple enough. Share owners receive a discount whenever they purchase (non-sale) items from the many different businesses that form Coles Myer: Kmart, Fosseys, Katies etc.

In the case of the ANZ, shareholders are now entitled to a range of benefits including fee-free bank cheques, discounts on home insurance and discounts for standard home loans (applies to an approval fee). There are other benefits such as reduced entry fees for unit trust, rollover and annuity investments, investment and superannuation bonds; discounts on scheduled brokerage rates on share purchases as well as free professional investment advisory services.

For certain people these benefits can amount to substantial savings. Indeed for a retiree who is perhaps managing an investment property (or two), with a self-managed superannuation fund and who is travelling overseas, the savings probably amount to many hundred of dollars. All for the investment of a parcel of ANZ shares. And it doesn't matter whether you are the owner of 100 or 10 000 shares, the same benefits apply.

NAB recently introduced its shareholder loyalty scheme. Some of the benefits include bonus interest on selected term deposits, fee-free transaction banking, and waiver of some establishment and ongoing fees on home loans. Only shareholders with 500 or more shares are eligible.

For the average person, however, the benefits are less clear. Certainly, a measure of benefit exists in the form of a 20 per cent discount on ANZ Home Insurance. That is, provided ANZ Home Insurance is competitive with its scheduled fees. But, there is, according to the earlier analysis in this chapter, a benefit in owning bank shares. Once again, it is not the intention of this book to offer investment advice. However, it is possible to make a double benefit from owning bank shares.

Although the other major bank companies have not as yet designed shareholder benefit schemes in the fashion of ANZ and NAB, all do pay dividends. And there are always long-term capital gain possibilities. For this decade at least owning bank shares has certainly been one way of beating the banks and profiting from it!

Investment rules

- Don't put all your eggs in one basket: especially the banks!
- People who cannot replace lost capital should invest in the safest and most secure investments.
- Ask for advice: search for the best adviser.
- Keep your emergency (liquid) funds in a cash management trust: they have consistently paid more than bank deposits for average amounts of money.
- Long-term investment funds must preserve their purchasing value: simple interest-bearing accounts on an after-tax basis will not achieve this.
- It is hard to beat the family home, first, and superannuation, second, as the most tax effective means of preserving your capital.
- Beat the banks by becoming a shareholder in them: there are privileges such as discounts on bank services — check them out.

Chapter 15

Some final words

A book just about banks would be difficult to read. So I take my hat off to the victims and heroes whose experiences add colour and life to these pages. They are ordinary people from all walks of life.

In terms of ordinary people achieving extraordinary things in their battles against the banks, John Symond's story must surely stand out. He took on the banks, recreating a modern version of *David and Goliath*. He operated on a simple formula applicable to all of us: do your homework and demand a better deal. If your bank won't give it to you, go elsewhere.

Our other heroes, while not achieving the notoriety of Symond, have certainly hit upon elegant solutions to everyday problems that affect all of us. Stephen Thaxter, our *banker without a bank account*, for example, proves there is indeed life after a cheque book and provides a lesson in good, sensible money management. 'By simply arranging for periodic payments and direct debits, I find no use at all for a cheque book.'

And then there was Erica, who did all her banking *bedside*. She hated queues and hated poor branch service even more. 'I never see the inside of a bank. I don't miss it at all.' More importantly she has simplified her banking to the point where she pays only a few dollars of fees each month.

And Phil, of course, is the very epitome of smart banking. Putting all his income direct into his mortgage, then (on a fee-free basis) drawing out what he needs to live on. 'You need to budget on the spending side, but I'm going to have my mortgage paid off in half the time.' Where else can you get the huge investment returns that early repayment of the home loan can deliver?

Arnold, who is a perfect example of the principle of *smart money* remained elusive while island hopping on his yacht. He did, however, make sure I heard his final word: 'Don't pay them a cent more than you need to. Put your money to work — not in the bank!'

Business banking represents a special challenge. Banks have been particularly intransigent when it comes to costs and charges on small to medium-sized business. Here we found Stan, who decided that self-funding, although requiring careful negotiations with suppliers and family, is a better option than bank debt for his fledgling business. 'I work hard for my money and I don't want the bank to get a penny more than they deserve.'

Finally, James, who saw that financial security meant good planning at a young age — budgets and investment — and who was prepared to invest time and energy into researching non-bank alternatives for his money. 'It was much smarter to invest money in the banks rather than with the banks. So that's what I did.'

Rather than continue to feel victimised and powerless all of our heroes took action. Apart from John Symond's, none of their actions is beyond the ability and reach of any individual. Most were motivated by a strong need to regain control of their own money. Some saw the injustices of the system and took their own private stand — Lee who paid all her bills in cash and in person remains defiant. But most needed to get control of their money. When they did so new opportunities unfolded for all of them.

All simplified their banking and looked for *smarter* ways to manage their money. All were enriched by their actions.

When we get off our collective backsides and start thinking about our banking and start shopping for better deals in all aspects of our finances — home loans, cheque accounts, savings accounts, credit cards, business loans — then the banks may collectively respond.

Meanwhile, by acting as individuals not only will we save money, but opportunities for creating financial independence will become available to us. By critically examining our need for the security of money in the bank we can remove some now antiquated myths about safety. We can feel empowered rather than small and inadequate.

A new era of banking is emerging. It is one which hands control back to the consumer with more choices and variety in how to deliver his or her own banking needs. But it is also one that guarantees more powerful banks with a new round of takeovers and mergers.

The juggernaut will crunch the unwitting — fewer branches and fee-for-service are the economic imperatives and will affect many people, particularly the elderly and the less informed. Competitive pressures may have undone the banks' stranglehold on the mortgage dollar but they still retain an iron grip on small and medium-sized business finance and credit cards. And they still control transaction accounts.

But the competition emerging on a number of fronts provides potential rewards for the shop-smart consumer who is prepared to step back from the confines of convenience and strive for a better deal.

Convenience plays a strong role in our relationship with the financial institutions. Many would still rather conduct both their shopping and their banking based solely on this. But with convenience comes a price. And the price is high, given the often topsy-like spending and banking habits of customers.

New age banking — telephone, ATM, Eftpos and the Internet — all deliver solutions for the convenience conscious. No more bank queues and no more fees — money can be moved over the phone.

Standing outside of the banks' own turf enables us to avoid the intimidation and irritation of dealing face-to-face with a system that never really cared for us. And in doing so, we can learn to care for ourselves — in a way that will bring joy, abundance and, best of all, empowerment.

Yearly Budget

Budgeting is often a confusing task. This guide makes it a very simple process. It offers an easy-to-complete, month-by-month annual budget sheet itemising your family income and expenditure.

INCOME (NET)	Jan	Feb	Mar	April	May
Salary/Wages	$	$	$	$	$
Dividends/Interest					
Other					
Total	$	$	$	$	$
EXPENDITURE Fixed					
Rent, Repayments (mortgage)	$	$	$	$	$
Rates – council					
– water					
Insurance – home					
– contents					
Electricity					
Gas					
Telephone					
Medical, hospital					
Life insurance or Disability					
Superannuation					
Hire purchase/Lease					
Loan repayments (other)					
School Fees					
Car – repayments					
– registration					
– insurance					
– licence fee					
Other					
Newspapers, etc.					
Subscriptions					
Essential					
Food					
Clothing					
Other					
Fares					
Petrol					
Car maintenance					
House maintenance					
Chemist					
Store accounts					
Other					
Non-essential					
Gifts					
Entertainment					
Sport					
Other (personal allowance)					
Holidays					
Sub-total					
Add 10% for miscellaneous					
Total	$	$	$	$	$
Overspent (Adjust from savings)	$	$	$	$	$
Surplus (Pay to savings)	$	$	$	$	$

Planner

It will help you understand your spending patterns and show you where surplus income could be used. A little time spent now will make planning a breeze in the future.

ne	July	Aug	Sept	Oct	Nov	Dec	TOTAL
	$	$	$	$	$	$	$
	$	$	$	$	$	$	$
	$	$	$	$	$	$	$
	$	$	$	$	$	$	$
	$	$	$	$	$	$	$
	$	$	$	$	$	$	$

Glossary

Bank jargon

Base lending rate: the rate which banks charge for their top blue-chip corporate customers.

Client margin: the addiitonal interest the banks charge for just about anybody else — up to 5 percentage points over the base rate if you are particularly undesirable.

Penalty rates: the additional interest the banks charge when you have either overdrawn your account, are late with a payment, or if a default has been triggered under a loan agreement. You could be up for an 8 percentage point surprise.

Honeymoon or introductory rate: the *come-in-sucker* rate before the real rate bites a year or so later.

Loyalty discounts: started by St George, who offer customers of five years or more a discount on their interest rate.

On-going fees: only $3 to $8 a month in the case of most home loans. But over a 25-year period it can add up.

Guarantee: a document signed by the third person — the guarantor, who then is liable for the debt plus *reasonable enforcement expenses*.

Unconscionable interest or charges: *excessive*, and usually relates to establishment fees, *exit* fees or prepaymennt fees.

Default: failure to meet debt payment on a due date.

Stepped interest rate: as the account increases the interest rate also increases. But the higher rate only applies to the higher part of the balance.

Directories

1 Where to find the latest information on interest rates

Market Faxts: market rates information service (02) 9247 6788

Market Choice: Internet service
http/www.mfaxts.com.au/bankchoice

Money Choices: a dial-up service provided by the Australian Consumers' Association 1900 1700 88

Metropolitan daily newspapers each Monday for a listing of principal bank deposit and lending rates.

On-line simulators and calculation tables:
http://www.hww.com.au/ymm

2 Where to find the latest information on the best mortgage deals

Loan Mart: independent financial advisers 02 9687 0055

Mortgage Choice 1800 64 6789

Money Choices (see above)

3 Where to get information on credit cards

Market Choice: Internet service (see above)

Money Choice: (see above)

Principal bank toll-free or national numbers:

Advance Bank	1800 818 762
ANZ	1800 035 500
Bank of Melbourne	1800 809 248

Commonwealth Bank	13 22 24
Metway Bank	1800 777 706
National Australia Bank	1800 630 600
Westpac	13 19 00

4 Where to go if you have a legitimate complaint against the bank

Australain Banking Industry Ombudsman	1 800 337 444
	(03) 9613 7333
	fax (03) 9613 7345

5 Other useful contacts

Australian Consumers' Association	(02) 9577 3333
Australian Pensioners' and Superannuants' Federation	(02) 9281 4566;
	fax (02) 9281 5951
Australians for Banking Justice	(02) 9365 1256
Consumer Credit Legal Centre	(02) 9698 9448
other states (WA and Vic.)	(09) 481 7662
	(03) 9670 5088
Credit Helpline	1800 808 488
Credit Reference Association of Australia	008 800 148
Credit Union of Australia	(07) 3365 0160
Departments of Consumer Affairs or Fair Trading	
Financial Planning Association	(03) 9614 2289
	fax (030) 9614 1912
	toll free 1800 337 301
National Centre on Retirement Investments	freecall 1800 020 110; (06) 281 5744
Superannuation Complaints Tribunal	13 14 34

Recommended reading

Making Money Made Simple, Noel Whittaker, Simon & Schuster Sydney, 1992.

Many editions have been published since the first edition was issued in the 1980s. Whittaker's book is comprehensive and easy to read. It presents a guide to investing and planning for retirement

The Woman's Money Book, Vivienne James, Anne O'Donovan, Melbourne, 1996.

A very user-friendly guide to sorting out your finances and putting your money where it works best.

Focus is a booklet issued by the credit unions; it is available at many credit union branches. It is useful for young people, offering them tips on savings, borrowing and buying a car.

Don't Kiss Your Money Goodbye is a joint publication by the Australian Securities Commssion and the Financial Planning Association of Australia Limited, 1995. The book gives investors advice on how to choose a financial adviser.

The Bold Riders: Behind Australia's corporate collapses, Trevor Sykes 2nd edn, Allen & Unwin, Sydney, 1996.

You Can Bank on the Wails: Bank Stories to make you smile, Peter Burke & Denis Hyde, Systex, Sydney, 1996.

Index